LONDON'S SPORTING HEROES

Map showing the London regions and the area covered in each chapter

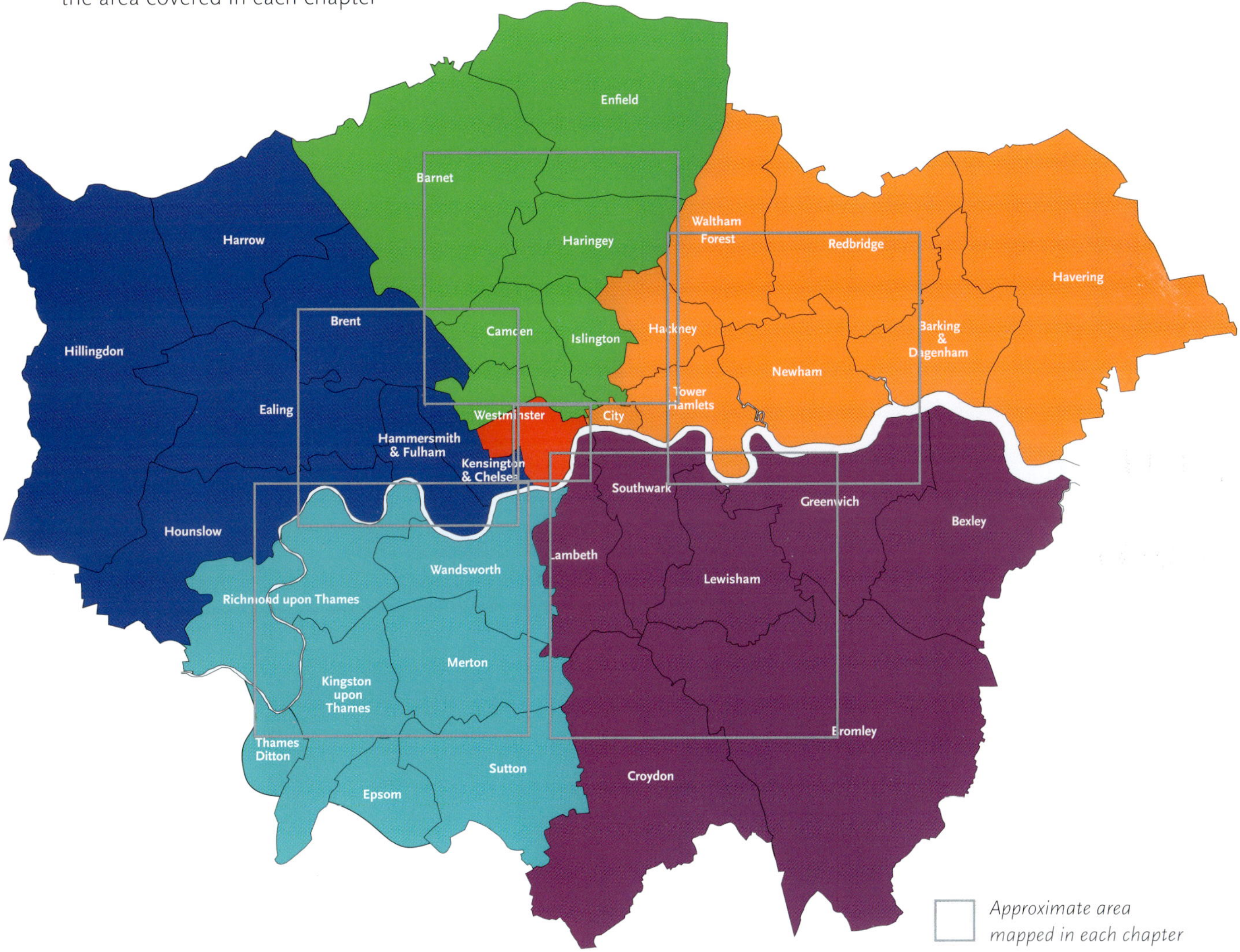

Enfield
Barnet
Harrow
Haringey
Waltham Forest
Redbridge
Havering
Brent
Camden
Islington
Hackney
Barking & Dagenham
Hillingdon
Ealing
Newham
Tower Hamlets
Westminster
City
Hammersmith & Fulham
Kensington & Chelsea
Southwark
Greenwich
Bexley
Hounslow
Wandsworth
Lambeth
Lewisham
Richmond upon Thames
Merton
Kingston upon Thames
Thames Ditton
Bromley
Sutton
Croydon
Epsom

Approximate area mapped in each chapter

Published in 2026 by Vision Sports Publishing

Vision Sports Publishing Ltd
19-23 High Street
Kingston upon Thames
Surrey
KT2 6PJ
visionsp.co.uk

ISBN 13: 978-1913412-83-8

Conceived and written by Ian Hewitt
Editor: Jim Drewett
Art director: Doug Cheeseman
Commercial director: Toby Trotman
Production editor: Ed Davis
Print production: Ulrika Drewett

Photography: Ian Hewitt, Sampson Lloyd, Jenifer Hewitt, Toby Trotman
Archive photography: Getty Images, Alamy, Historic England, All England Lawn Tennis Club

Printed and bound in the UK by Bell & Bain

This product is made of FSC®-certified and other controlled material

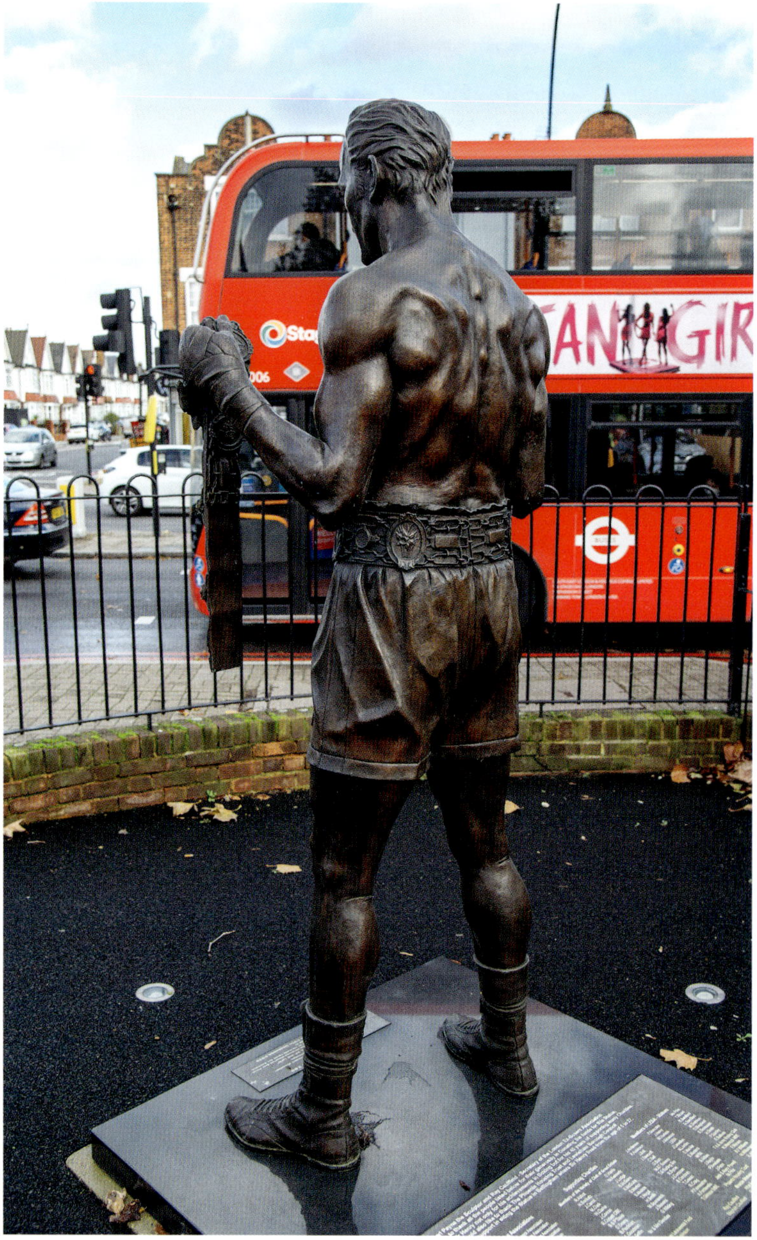

CONTENTS

Left: A compelling statue of boxing legend Henry Cooper watches over a busy junction in Bellingham, south-east London

Introduction

Exploring the capital's rich sporting heritage

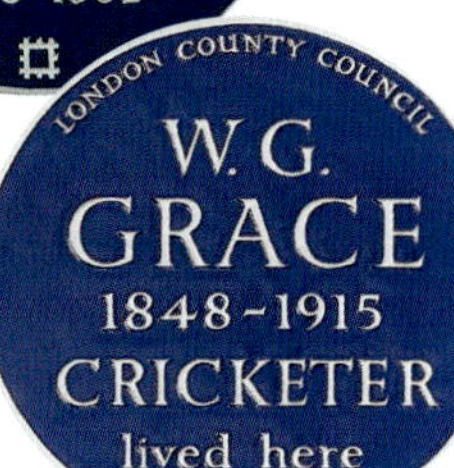

The aim of this book is to share a journey of discovery, learning and celebration.

London is, joyfully, a sporting capital of the world. Many major sports have their formative roots in Britain – with London at the centre. The first city to stage three modern Olympic Games, it is the home of iconic – and thriving – sporting venues revered throughout the world and is steeped in sporting heritage.

Our principal focus in this book is to recall and celebrate sporting heroes commemorated by plaques, statues and murals around London – nearly all being individuals who were born in the capital or lived here for an important period of their lives.

Many of those celebrated are renowned greats of sport. Others are less well known but have nevertheless shaped sport in important ways. It is these stories that so often provide, unexpectedly, new learning and delight for the explorer. All have contributed to the sporting history of London.

Although there may be many outstanding individuals who are not (at least as yet) immortalised in plaques, statues and murals, I believe those that are and feature on these pages offer a fascinating insight into London's deep sporting history.

The blue plaque scheme run by English Heritage since 1986 (taking over from the Greater London Council and originally the Royal Society of Arts) is the most established and respected, although several London boroughs or authorities have their own schemes. Other organisations and clubs – including the Royal Mail (with their gold-painted post boxes celebrating London 2012 Olympic champions) – have also been proud to commemorate particular heroes. More informally, vibrantly painted murals (often football-themed) have provided a different medium through which to celebrate both local and national sporting heroes.

This collection of London's sporting plaques, statues and murals is presented by

A vibrant mural near Wembley Stadium features England's Lionesses – here, Alessia Russo – in celebration during their victorious Euro 2022 campaign

Post boxes like this one in Westminster were painted gold by Royal Mail to commemorate local Team GB gold medallists at the London Olympic and Paralympic Games 2012

region, with each offering a diverse range of heroes and history. Readers may not physically conduct a series of tours, but I hope that this approach will at least encourage enquiry or curiosity as to whom or what (often surprisingly) can be found around the streets and byways of our great city.

London for the purposes of this publication means the administrative area of Greater London, covering its 32 London boroughs and the City of London (but adding Epsom and Thames Ditton in the south-west for convenience). The sub-division into six regions is not formal but pragmatic.

Importantly, many archive photographs relevant to a particular sport, event or individual are included to help trigger a visual image and build a better understanding of the context in which the individual lived and played or a sporting event took place.

Sporting history adds richness and context – as well as insight into many developments in society that have shaped sport over the years. I hope this book will enable readers to discover, learn and enjoy more of that history through the kaleidoscope of heroes who have contributed to London's unparalleled sporting heritage.

Ian Hewitt, author

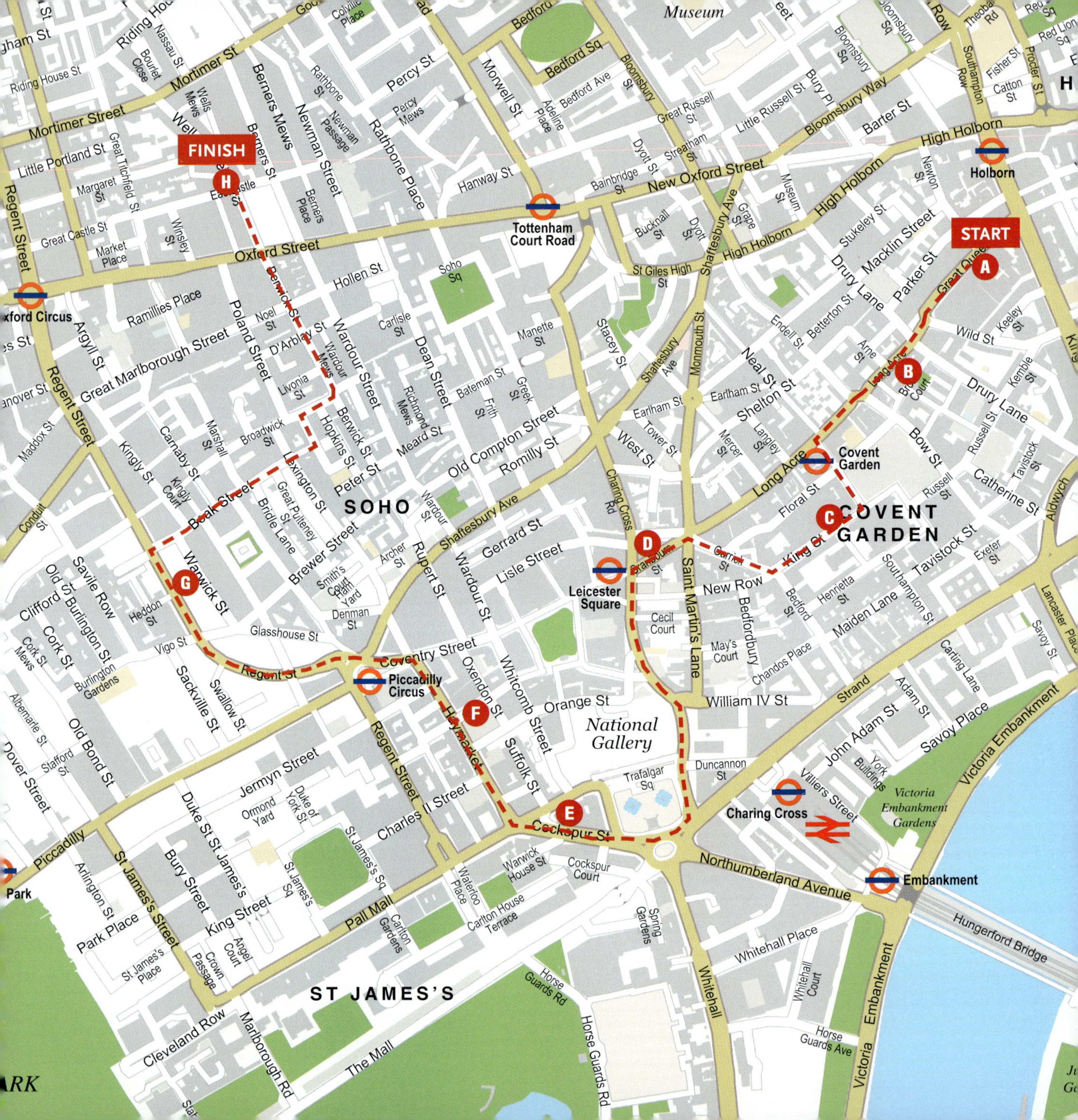

START
A
B
C
D
E
F
G
H
FINISH
Museum
Holborn
Tottenham Court Road
Oxford Circus
Covent Garden
Leicester Square
Piccadilly Circus
Charing Cross
Embankment
SOHO
COVENT GARDEN
ST JAMES'S
National Gallery
Trafalgar Sq
Victoria Embankment Gardens
Oxford Street
New Oxford Street
High Holborn
Mortimer Street
Little Portland St
Great Castle St
Margaret St
Market Place
Winsley St
Eastcastle St
Berners St
Berners Mews
Newman Street
Rathbone Place
Percy St
Hanway St
Bedford Sq
Bedford Ave
Morwell St
Adeline Place
Bloomsbury St
Bloomsbury Way
Great Russell St
Little Russell St
Bury Pl
Barter St
Southampton Row
Dyott St
Streatham St
Bainbridge St
Bucknall St
Museum St
Shaftesbury Ave
St Giles High St
Grape St
Stukeley St
Macklin Street
Drury Lane
Parker St
Great Queen St
Wild St
Keeley St
Kemble St
Endell St
Betterton St
Arne St
Long Acre
Neal St
Shelton St
Earlham St
Monmouth St
Mercer St
Langley St
Bow St
Russell St
Catherine St
Floral St
King St
Garrick St
New Row
Bedford St
Henrietta St
Southampton St
Tavistock St
Exeter St
Maiden Lane
Chandos Place
Bedfordbury
May's Court
Cecil Court
Saint Martin's Lane
William IV St
Strand
Adam St
John Adam St
Savoy Place
Villiers Street
York Buildings
Duncannon St
Victoria Embankment
Northumberland Avenue
Hungerford Bridge
Whitehall
Whitehall Place
Whitehall Court
Horse Guards Ave
Horse Guards Rd
Spring Gardens
Cockspur St
Cockspur Court
Warwick House St
Carlton House Terrace
Waterloo Place
Carlton Gardens
Pall Mall
The Mall
Marlborough Rd
Cleveland Row
St James's Place
Park Place
St James's Street
Crown Passage
Angel Court
King Street
St James's Sq
Bury Street
Duke St St James's
Ormond Yard
Duke of York St
Jermyn Street
Charles II Street
Regent Street
Haymarket
Suffolk St
Whitcomb Street
Orange St
Oxendon St
Coventry Street
Piccadilly
Arlington St
Dover Street
Albemarle St
Stafford St
Old Bond St
Sackville St
Swallow St
Vigo St
Burlington Gardens
Cork St
Clifford St
Old Burlington St
Savile Row
Heddon St
Glasshouse St
Warwick St
Denman St
Smith's Court
Ham Yard
Archer St
Rupert St
Wardour St
Gerrard St
Lisle Street
Charing Cross Rd
Cranbourn St
West St
Tower St
Stacey St
Manette St
Greek St
Frith St
Bateman St
Dean Street
Romilly St
Old Compton Street
Meard St
Richmond Mews
Carlisle St
Soho Sq
Hollen St
Berwick St
Peter St
Hopkins St
Lexington St
Brewer Street
Great Pulteney St
Bridle Lane
Beak Street
Broadwick St
Marshall St
Carnaby St
Kingly Court
Kingly St
Livonia St
D'Arblay St
Noel St
Poland Street
Great Marlborough Street
Ramillies Place
Argyll St
Conduit St
Maddox St
Hanover St
Great Titchfield St
Riding House St
Wells Mews
Nassau St
Bourlet Close
Riding House St
Colville Place
Percy Mews
Rathbone St
Newman Passage
Berners Place
Newton St
Theobalds Rd
Fisher St
Catton St
Procter St
Red Lion Sq
Bloomsbury Sq
Aldwych
Lancaster Place
Savoy St
Carting Lane
Park

A sporting walk in Central London

Distance: 2 miles. Time: Approx. 1 to 1 1/2 hours

This walk is the perfect introduction to the rich sporting history that can be discovered in Britain's capital city. For more detailed information on each location, consult the Central London chapter.

A 63 Great Queen Street, WC2

We start outside the Connaught Rooms where a plaque commemorates a meeting in 1863 which led to the formation of the **Football Association**, a watershed in the history of the world's most universal game.

See 3 *page 16*

B 75 Long Acre, WC2

0.1 mile approx. 3 mins

In Long Acre we discover the site of **Dennis Johnson**'s workshop where, in the early 19th century, he invented and sold Britain's first bicycle.

See 4 *page 17*

C 43 King Street WC2

0.2 miles approx. 5 mins

Next, we head to Covent Garden to locate the former site of the **National Sporting Club**, founded in 1891. The de facto governing body of boxing until the 1920s, this was 'the home of modern glove boxing' where bouts were held after dinner.

See 5 *page 18*

D 21 Cranbourn Street, WC2

0.2 miles approx. 4 mins

Close to one of the entrances to Leicester Square station, distinctive signage recalls the former site of **John Wisden**'s 'cricket and cigar' shop. *Wisden Cricketers' Almanack*, founded in 1864, is 'the Bible of Cricket' and the longest running annual publication in sport.

See 6 *page 20*

E 1 Cockspur Street, SW1

0.4 miles approx. 9 mins

At the former site of the distinguished Pall Mall Restaurant, a plaque recalls an historic meeting in 1871 when representatives of many London football clubs, unwilling to join the 'no-hacking', round-ball game of the Football Association, formed the **Rugby Football Union**.

See 7 *page 22*

F 36 Panton Street SW1

0.2 mile approx. 5 mins

An ideal stop for some welcome refreshment, the pub still known as the **Tom Cribb** is where the champion prize-fighter of the early 19th century ran a tavern after his retirement. Inside, plaques and memorabilia commemorate the fighter and another plaque outside recalls the extraordinary story of **Bill Richmond**, the world's first sports star of African heritage.

See 8 *page 24*

G 128 Regent Street W1

0.4 miles approx. 9 mins

Next we discover the place where, in 1892, Lord Stanley – then the Governor General of Canada – purchased the decorative bowl which would become the world-famous trophy for ice hockey's **Stanley Cup**.

See 10 *page 28*

H 12/13 Wells Street W1

0.5 mile approx. 13 mins

Finally, we arrive at The Champion pub where we can enjoy a delightful collection of stained glass windows celebrating 'champions' of the late 19th and early 20th century including cricketer **WG Grace**, tennis player **William Renshaw** and jockey **Fred Archer**.

See 9 *page 26*

CENTRAL LONDON

Henry Segrave, speed world record holder on land and water after the First World War, lived in Central London. It is here, in Marylebone, that a plaque commemorates this national hero.

CENTRAL LONDON

Our tour of discovery starts in Central London. The areas of Holborn, Covent Garden, Westminster, Belgravia and Pimlico were at the very heart of the capital in the 19th century. These locations witnessed important episodes in the history of a wide range of sporting institutions, individuals and events – none more important than the landmark meetings that resulted in the formation of the Football Association and the Rugby Football Union.

Commemorative plaques identify the former homes of many trailblazers in a variety of sports, including cycling, aviation, tennis, table tennis and motor racing. Taverns – some in which pints are still poured – were sites for planning and celebration by the prize-fighting fraternity of the 18th and 19th centuries.

Let us share a journey as we discover a fascinating range of sporting pathfinders and leaders who have been recognised in plaque or bronze, sometimes for distinguished contributions to society in fields beyond sport. There will almost certainly be some surprises along the way and some unexpected locations.

1. John Jaques III
2. William Webb Ellis
3. Ebenezer Cobb Morley and the Football Association
4. Denis Johnson
5. National Sporting Club
6. John Wisden
7. Rugby Football Union
8. Tom Cribb and Bill Richmond
9. The Champion:
William Renshaw, Fred Archer, WG Grace
10. Lord Stanley of Preston
11. Quintin Hogg
12. Sir Henry Segrave
13. Sir Thomas Sopwith
14. Sir Francis Chichester
15. Jack Broughton
16. Sir Roger Bannister
17. Olympic golden post box
18. Harry Mallin
19. Walter Wingfield
20. Arthur Haygarth
21. Lord Philip Noel-Baker

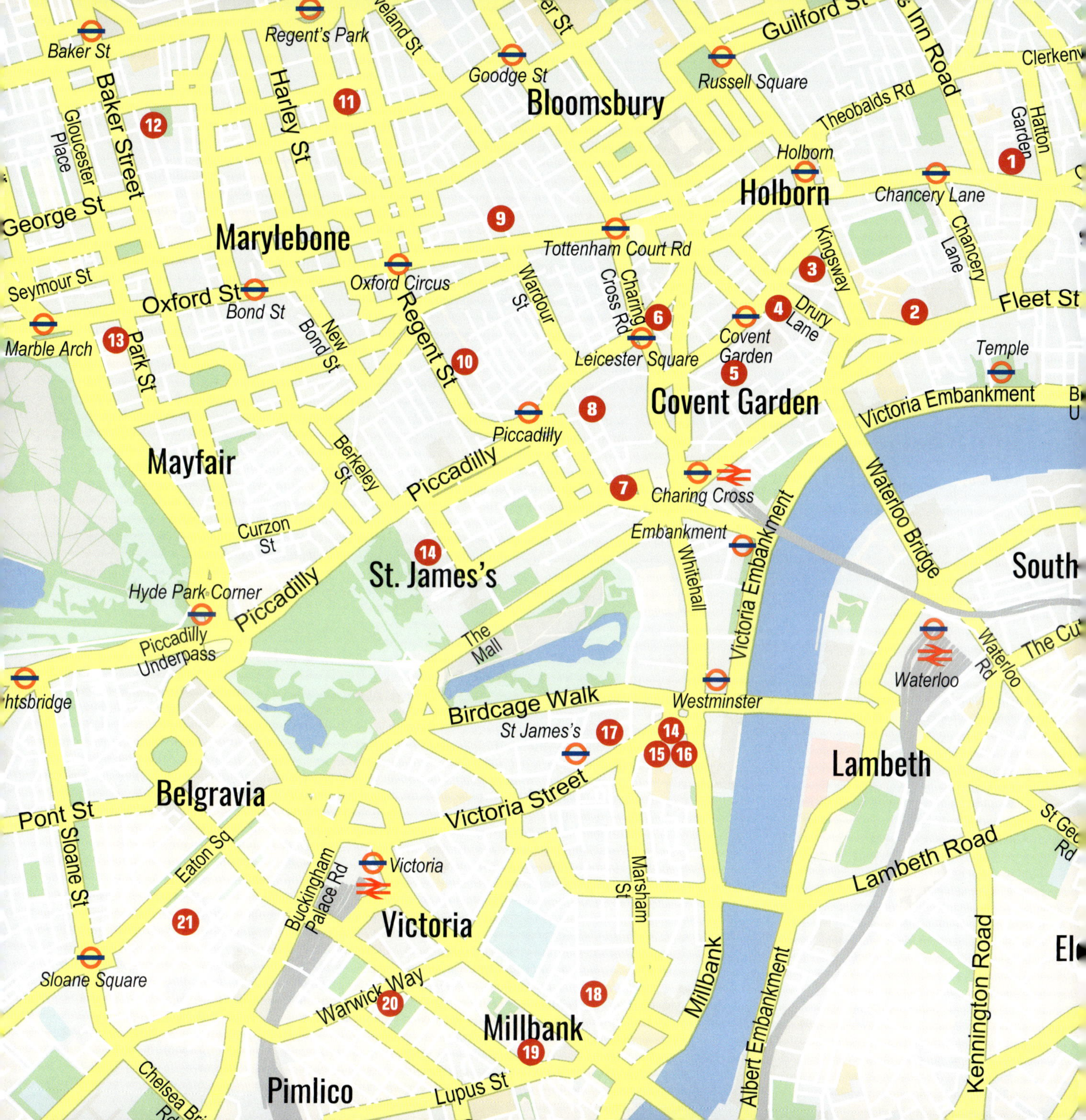

Baker St
Regent's Park
Goodge St
Guilford St
Russell Square
Clerkenwell
Bloomsbury
Theobalds Rd
Hatton Garden
Gloucester Place
Baker Street
Harley St
Holborn
Chancery Lane
George St
Marylebone
Tottenham Court Rd
Kingsway
Chancery Lane
Seymour St
Oxford St
Bond St
Oxford Circus
Wardour St
Charing Cross Rd
Drury Lane
Fleet St
Marble Arch
Park St
New Bond St
Regent St
Leicester Square
Covent Garden
Temple
Covent Garden
Victoria Embankment
Berkeley St
Piccadilly
Mayfair
Piccadilly
Charing Cross
Waterloo Bridge
Curzon St
Embankment
St. James's
Whitehall
Victoria Embankment
South
Hyde Park Corner
Piccadilly
The Mall
Piccadilly Underpass
Waterloo Rd
The Cut
Waterloo
Westminster
Birdcage Walk
St James's
Lambeth
Belgravia
Victoria Street
Pont St
Sloane St
Eaton Sq
Buckingham Palace Rd
Victoria
Marsham St
Lambeth Road
Victoria
Sloane Square
Warwick Way
Millbank
Albert Embankment
Kennington Road
Millbank
Pimlico
Lupus St
Chelsea Bri Rd
1
2
3
4
5
6
7
8
9
10
11
12
13
14
14
15
16
17
18
19
20
21

1

John Jaques III

1860 – 1877

Bounce Farringdon, 121 Holborn, Holborn

EC1N 2TD

We start in Holborn, where we recall the beginnings of a sport that was created – and indeed is still being played – on this very site.

With the growing popularity of lawn tennis in the 1880s, many tried to develop an indoor version – often as an after-dinner parlour game. The Jaques family company launched a game using drum-type bats, a cork ball and a foot-high net. Others marketed variations. Names used included 'Whiff-Waff' and 'Ping-Pong' (derived, apparently, from the sound of cork-wrapped balls on the skin bats and the table).

The discovery of the celluloid ball around 1900 was game-changing. John Jaques III re-introduced his company's game, which was now marketed – jointly with Hamley Brothers' store – under the trademark 'Ping-Pong'. The game became a craze in Victorian society. The first World Table Tennis Championships were held in 1926 in London. A Victorian parlour game had turned into an international sport. Inside the Bounce Farringdon venue, but sadly no longer on open display, a plaque proudly proclaims that on this site ping pong was created and patented by John Jaques III in 1901 (although no specific patent has been discovered).

Perhaps coincidentally, perhaps not, the site is now a modern bar and activity venue where you can play the very game that began here. At the London Olympic Games in 2012, Boris Johnson (then Mayor of London) memorably proclaimed of the British: "We looked at a dining table and saw the opportunity to play whiff-waff. That is why London is the sporting capital of the world."

Right: An illustration of English high society playing the newly fashionable game of 'Ping-Pong' in the early 20th century

Below: Table tennis is still being played at 'Bounce' on the very site where the game was created

CENTRAL

A Victorian parlour game turned into an international sport

2

William Webb Ellis

1806 – 1872

St Clement Danes, Strand, Westminster

WC2R 1DH

WILLIAM WEBB ELLIS
Rector 1843-1855 who at Rugby School in 1823 with a fine disregard for the rules of football as played in his time first took the ball in his arms and ran

Did one moment in 1823 change the course of a sport? A wall plaque inside St Clement Danes Church commemorates the instant when, legend has it, rugby was born.

There was no clear distinction between the games we now know as soccer and rugby before the emergence of a form of 'football' without 'hacking' (kicking an opponent in the shins) led to the formation of the Football Association in 1863. A group of London clubs, refusing to adopt the new Football Association's rules, met in 1871 and decided to establish the Rugby Football Union in response.

Many years later, keen to demonstrate that their game had a long tradition, ex-students of Rugby School discovered an article, written in 1880, recording an incident more than 50 years earlier involving a 17-year-old pupil playing football there. Apparently, during a match William Webb Ellis had caught the ball. He should have stepped back and kicked ahead. Instead, "Ellis, for the first time, disregarded this rule... and rushed forwards with the ball in his hands towards the opposite goal."

Right: An illustration from c1880 depicts the 'carrying' game of rugby football

Below: St Clement Danes church in Aldwych, where William Webb Ellis was rector

CENTRAL

This moment has come to symbolise the birth of rugby football. But why is it celebrated here in the Strand? Webb Ellis, who so far as we know never mentioned the incident, went into the church and became the rector at St Clement Danes. The wall plaque here celebrates that alleged iconic moment of enthusiasm (or cunning) in 1823.

Webb Ellis never mentioned the incident and went on to become a rector

3

Ebenezer Cobb Morley and the Football Association

1831 – 1924

63 Great Queen Street, Covent Garden

WC2B 5DA

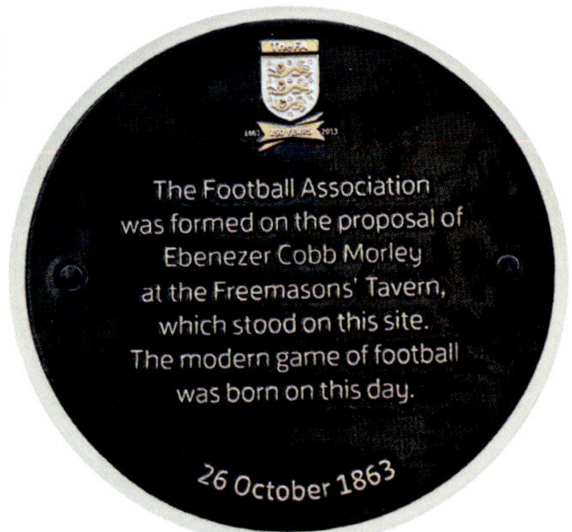

Moving to Covent Garden, outside the Connaught Rooms in Great Queen Street, we find a plaque commemorating a watershed meeting in 1863.

As the 19th century progressed, young men often sought to continue the ball games they had played at public school or university. Each institution, however, had its own rules and traditions. Early attempts to devise a compromise set of 'football' rules had only modest success. Then, on 26 October 1863, representatives from clubs formed in the London area held a meeting at the Freemasons' Tavern in Covent Garden. The meeting was led by Ebenezer Cobb Morley, a Yorkshireman living in London and the captain of the Barnes football team. The group called themselves the Football Association and agreed the basis on which they would play "association football". Rules, drafted by Morley, were eventually agreed. One rule simply said: "No player shall run with the ball." Morley became the first Secretary, and later President.

In 2015 a plaque was placed in Great Queen Street, near the site where Morley and the other 'founding fathers' held their landmark gathering. They surely could not have anticipated that their game would become the world's most universal sport.

CENTRAL

Formed here, association football would go on to become the world's most popular game

The Freemasons' Tavern, Great Queen Street, as it would have looked when the Football Association was founded there in 1863

4

Denis Johnson

c1760 – 1833

75 Long Acre, Covent Garden

WC2E 9JS

Denis Johnson's 'hobby horse', with its wooden frame, was the first bicycle made and sold in Britain

Staying in Covent Garden, in Long Acre we come across a key location in the beginnings of cycling in the early 1800s. It was from a workshop on this site that coachmaker Denis Johnson made and sold Britain's first bicycle.

Johnson had created an improved version of an earlier form of two-wheel vehicle invented in Germany (by Karl Drais and known as a Draisine). Johnson's version, patented in London in 1818, featured an elegantly curved wooden frame which enabled the use of larger wooden wheels. Several parts were made of metal, making the vehicle lighter than the continental version. He called it a 'pedestrian curricle' or 'velocipede' but it was popularly known as a 'hobby horse'. The rider, striking his or her feet alternately on the ground, could now stride and move swiftly.

It was here that Denis Johnson made and sold Britain's first bicycle

Johnson made around 300 of these bicycles and his marketing skills led to his 'hobby horse' becoming fashionable in London society.

Here, in Long Acre, a plaque erected by the City of Westminster records the site of Johnson's landmark invention. Two centuries later, cycling would be the sport of many great British Olympic champions.

CENTRAL

5

National Sporting Club

1891 – 1929

43 King Street, Covent Garden

WC2E 8JY

A green plaque on the wall of a building in King Street, opposite Covent Garden Market, marks the former location of the National Sporting Club, which played a leading role in promoting boxing as a respectable sport as it moved from the era of bare-knuckle pugilists.

Founded in 1891 as a private members' club, bouts took place after dinner and were fought in silence. It was here that the 'Queensberry Rules' (first introduced by John Graham Chambers in 1867 and endorsed by the Marquis of Queensberry) were generally accepted as regulating the sport of boxing (including three-minute rounds, gloves of good quality, no wrestling and 10 seconds for a knockout) and then further developed.

The National Sporting Club became the de facto governing body of the sport. In 1909, the club's president – the 5th Earl of Lonsdale – introduced the Lonsdale Belt as a prize to the British champion at each weight class. Its lasting prestige has continued to this day.

By the 1920s larger venues, open to the public, competed to meet spectator demand. The club closed its premises in Covent Garden and moved elsewhere. A plaque, erected by the City of Westminster in 2015, celebrates the National Sporting Club as "the home of modern glove boxing".

Right: A painting depicting the scene following a boxing match at the National Sporting Club in 1919 with Welshman Jimmy Wilde being congratulated by the Prince of Wales (later Edward VIII)

Left: The former home of the National Sporting Club in the heart of Covent Garden

CENTRAL

Founded in 1891 as a private members' club, bouts took place after dinner and were fought in silence

6

John Wisden

1826 – 1884

21 Cranbourn Street, Covent Garden

WC2H 7AA

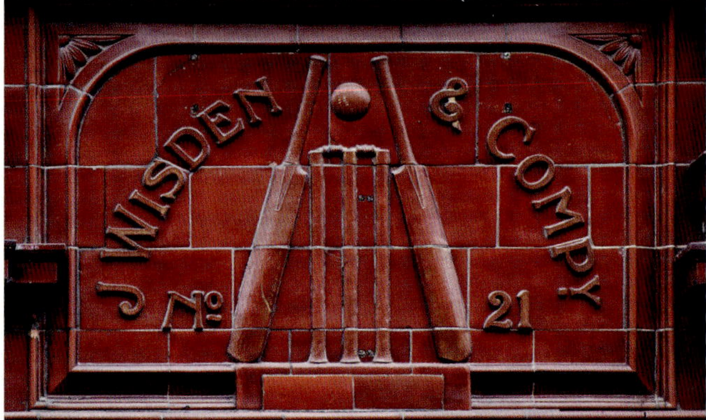

Incongruously positioned above a takeaway food shop in Cranbourn Street, next to one of the entrances to Leicester Square underground station, a decorative wall sign carries a name synonymous with cricket.

John Wisden was a good all-round cricketer, nicknamed 'the Little Marvel', but better known now for the *Wisden Cricketers' Almanack*. The 'Bible of Cricket' was first published in 1864, after he had retired from playing. The groundbreaking work, with its famous yellow cover, is still the most respected source of key statistics and records relating to the game. The longest-running annual publication in sport, the work has grown substantially under a series of editors and owners and its annual publication remains a major yearly event.

Wisden is a name synonymous with cricket

Wisden had started a cricket equipment business in Leamington Spa in 1850 and five years later opened a 'cricket and cigar' shop in central London. It moved to Cranbourn Steet in 1872. The enterprise continued after his death and became an international sports business.

At the former shop location, this distinctive sign – with its arrangement of cricket bats, stumps and ball – is incorporated into the tiled frontage of the underground station. It is a delightful reminder of Wisden's permanent association with cricket.

Above: The decorative frontage above John Wisden's former shop in Cranbourn Street

Below: Published annually since 1864, the Wisden Cricketers' Almanack is famous for its distinctive yellow cover

CENTRAL

Passers-by near Leicester Square engage in daily street life below the frontage of John Wisden's former shop

7

Rugby Football Union

1871

1 Cockspur Street, Westminster

SW1Y 5DL

In Cockspur Street, at the junction with Pall Mall East, a wall plaque commemorates another legendary meeting in the history of sport.

It is here, on 26 January 1871, that representatives from 21 clubs who played 'the rugby-type game' (including carrying and tackling) met at a hostelry then known as the Pall Mall Restaurant. The purpose was to develop a common 'code of practice' for the game separate from the unacceptable, no hacking, round-ball game of the Football Association, which had been formed eight years earlier. The plaque outside the building (the restaurant has long since gone) marks the location of this founding meeting of the Rugby Football Union.

Rules, drawn up by three former students of Rugby School, were agreed by the following June, by which time the first international match had been held (Scotland defeating England in Edinburgh).

The game in 1871 was very different from today. There were 20 players on each side, mostly forwards. Ironically, hacking and tripping were abolished. Handling was allowed but passing was not encouraged. The game would develop further, but the

Above: The stone plaque recording the landmark meeting at the then Pall Mall Restaurant in 1871

Below: The centenary of the RFU's formation was celebrated in stamp by Royal Mail in 1971

CENTRAL

The purpose was to develop a common 'code of practice' separate from the round-ball game of the Football Association

foundations of rugby union as we know it today had been established.

The clubs present at the meeting included well-known names such as Blackheath, Richmond, Wellington College and Harlequins. One notable absentee was the representative from Wasps. Accounts vary as to the reason for his absence, including a suggestion that he spent too much time at the wrong public house.

A painting depicts an early international rugby match between Scotland and England in Edinburgh in 1886

8

Tom Cribb

1781 – 1848

Bill Richmond

1763 – 1829

36 Panton Street, St. James's

SW1Y 4EA

Moving to Panton Street, we recall a bare-knuckle champion of the early 19th century. Tom Cribb's name continues to resonate in London – including here through the Tom Cribb public house on the site where the fighter ran a hostelry after his retirement. A blue plaque commemorating Cribb was erected by English Heritage in 2005, and a nearby brass counterpart provides further background.

Cribb's exploits were widely reported in the new weekly newspapers at the time. Recognised as English champion in 1809, he reigned undefeated until his retirement in 1822. Cribb fought a legendary fight in 1810 against Tom Molineaux, a former slave freed from a plantation in Virginia and regarded as the champion of America. It was, in effect, a fight to be world champion. Finally, after 35 rounds of a brutal and controversial contest, an exhausted Molineaux declared, "Me can fight no more" and collapsed.

Cribb's reputation was nationwide. A prominent society figure, he was invited by George IV to be an usher at the King's coronation in 1821. After retirement, his fortunes deteriorated. He was nevertheless buried with nobility, and his distinctive tomb still stands prominently in St Mary's Gardens in Woolwich (*see South-East London*).

Above: Plaques at the Tom Cribb public house tell the story of the great prize-fighter

Below: An illustration of Tom Cribb's second fight with the Virginian Tom Molineaux – with Bill Richmond as one of Cribb's seconds

In 1810, Cribb effectively became the first-ever 'world champion' fighter

CENTRAL

Left: *Bill Richmond, c1805, who had been freed from slavery and brought to England by Lord Percy*

Below: A BBC History plaque outside the Tom Cribb pub recalls Richmond's last evening

Lingering at the Tom Cribb, another plaque outside the well-known public house recalls Bill Richmond – one of the world's first sports stars of African heritage.

Born into slavery in Staten Island, New York, he was seen in a tavern brawl involving British soldiers during the American War of Independence by Hugh Percy, 2nd Duke of Northumberland and a commander of British forces in the city. Percy, an abolitionist, arranged for Richmond's freedom and ensured that, upon moving to Britain in 1777, he received an education and an apprenticeship.

Aged 40, Richmond took-up bare-knuckle fighting, becoming one of England's leading pugilists and earning then-unprecedented acclaim for a black sportsman. Good friends with Tom Cribb, he was also invited to be an usher at the coronation of King George IV. He died while visiting Cribb at his Panton Street hostelry.

Inside the modern pub hangs a portrait of Richmond along with a fascinating summary of his extraordinary life.

Bill Richmond was one of the world's first sports stars of African heritage

9

The Champion

12/13 Wells Street, Fitzrovia

W1T 3PA

Refreshment is also enjoyed at The Champion public house in Wells Street. Inside, stained glass windows, crafted by artist Ann Sotheran in 1989, depict an array of sporting heroes. Among the prominent sporting figures of the Victorian and Edwardian period celebrated, three giants stand out.

William Renshaw (1861–1904) was Wimbledon's first great tennis champion. Born in Leamington Spa, he later moved to Kensington. With an aggressive serving, smashing and volleying style, he won the singles title seven times (a record only surpassed in 2017 by Roger Federer). Renshaw and his brother, Ernest, were also five-time winners of the gentlemen's doubles. Having won the singles title three times in succession from 1881, he became owner of the trophy and the All England Club purchased a new Challenge Cup. Renshaw promptly won the next three Championships and became owner of the replacement silverware. The Club learned its lesson and now owns the Wimbledon trophy in perpetuity.

Another window celebrates **Fred Archer** (1857–1886). Top jockeys were amongst the Victorian era's best-known sportsmen, and Archer was the most famous of them all. Champion jockey for 13 consecutive seasons, beginning in 1874 at the age of 17, he rode an astonishing 2,748 winners, with 21 Classic victories including five Derby wins at Epsom. He tragically committed suicide, aged just 29, during a period of delirium and depression after the deaths of his wife and son in childbirth. He remains a legend of the sport.

The other great sporting figure celebrated is **WG Grace** (1848–1915). Known as 'the Champion' and 'the Great Cricketer', his extraordinary career is featured elsewhere (*see West London and South-East London*).

This is a splendid place for refreshment and to ponder the achievements of these sporting heroes of their time.

Above: Sporting surroundings enrich the interior of The Champion

Right: Impressive stained glass windows celebrate sporting greats William Renshaw, Fred Archer and WG Grace

Raise a glass to British sporting greats at The Champion pub

CENTRAL

10

Lord Stanley of Preston

1841 – 1908

128 Regent Street, Soho

W1B 5SD

We move to Regent Street, at the corner with Regent Place, where a wall plaque connects us with a great sporting trophy – but, surprisingly, one that is more famous on the other side of the Atlantic.

The trophy in question is presented to the winners of the annual ice hockey championship series in North America known famously as the 'Stanley Cup'. It was from a silversmith on this site, GR Collis & Co. (now Boodles), that Lord Stanley of Preston purchased the original trophy in 1892.

Stanley was appointed as Governor General of Canada in 1888. There, he became keen on ice hockey, which was in its infancy as an organised sport. His son, Arthur, suggested that his father donate a trophy as "an outward and visible sign of the hockey championship". Bearing an inscription that reads 'Dominion Hockey Challenge Cup', the Stanley Cup was first presented in 1893 and is North America's oldest professional sports trophy. Lifting it is now the prime goal of teams (both Canadian and American) in the National Hockey League.

An impressive decorative bowl, the silverware was made in Sheffield and purchased for 10 guineas. A silver and nickel copy of the bowl now tops a distinctively tall plinth – featuring the names of the winning teams – and is awarded to each season's champions, while the original bowl resides in the Hockey Hall of Fame in Toronto.

Above: The original bowl of the Stanley Cup, acquired in Regent Street in 1892

Below: The Stanley Cup, with its towering base, is joyfully lifted by the 1974 winners, the Philadelphia Flyers

CENTRAL

The Stanley Cup, the famous ice hockey trophy, was first acquired in London

11

Quintin Hogg

1845 – 1903

Portland Place, Marylebone

W1B 1PT

Many philanthropic individuals and religious organisations in late Victorian society advocated sport as a way to develop well-being and moral character – the so-called doctrine of 'muscular Christianity'. One was Quintin Hogg, who is immortalised with a striking monument in Portland Place, opposite BBC Broadcasting House.

Sculpted by George Frampton and erected in 1906, the Quintin and Alice Hogg Memorial captures the noble ideals of the well-known philanthropist (grandfather of a later leading British politician) and his wife. Keen on sport and especially football (having made two appearances for Scotland), Hogg strongly believed that combining physical culture and education offered young working men a path to self-improvement. Hogg is depicted with a bible in hand and flanked by two youths, one bearing a football.

The memorial is a listed Grade II monument and a London landmark.

Hogg was a passionate advocate of physical culture and education as the path to self-improvement

12

Sir Henry Segrave

1896 – 1930

6 St Andrew's Mansions, Dorset Street, Marylebone

W1U 4EQ

Tall, handsome and talented, Henry Segrave was Britain's great figure during the heroic age of speed in the years after the First World War and the first person to hold both the land and water speed records at the same time.

During the war, Segrave attained the rank of Major. After being demobbed and while living in a ground-floor flat in St Andrew's Mansions in Marylebone, he started motor racing at the Brooklands racing circuit. Success came quickly. Joining the Sunbeam-Talbot-Darracq team in 1921, he won the French Grand Prix, becoming the first British driver to win in continental Europe driving a British-built car.

Segrave then gave up motor racing in order to challenge the speed records. He first broke the world land speed record at Southport Sands in Lancashire in 1926. He subsequently broke the land record twice more – reaching over 231 mph at Daytona Beach, Florida, in a renowned car named Golden Arrow. Segrave subsequently turned to water. In 1930, shortly after being knighted, he broke the water

Henry Segrave was Britain's great figure in a heroic age of speed

A portrait of national hero Henry Segrave from the 1920s

CENTRAL

speed record, averaging 98.76 mph over two runs on Lake Windermere. On the third run, the boat capsized at full speed and Segrave was fatally injured. The nation mourned the tragedy, described in the press as "a heavy loss to England and the Empire".

The Segrave Trophy has since been awarded, in his honour, by the Royal Automobile Club to a British national who demonstrates 'Outstanding Skill, Courage and Initiative on Land, Water and in the Air'.

Erected in 2009 by English Heritage, a blue plaque on the wall at St Andrew's Mansions in W1 marks where Segrave lived for four years as he began his extraordinary racing career.

Golden Arrow, Segrave's famous car, en route to Selfridges to go on display after the land speed record was broken in 1929

13

Sir Thomas Sopwith

1888 – 1989

46 Green Street, Mayfair

W1K 7FY

A wall plaque in Green Street, Mayfair, identifies the former home of the extraordinary Thomas Sopwith, the pioneering aviator and aircraft manufacturer who embraced a relentless pursuit of adventure in the early years of the 20th century.

Born in Kensington and educated at an engineering college, 'Tommy' Sopwith became fascinated by all forms of transport, many of which were in their infancy. It was ultimately the new and dangerous world of aviation that captured his inventive talents. Learning to fly in 1910, he crashed on his first flight after a journey of 300 yards. Shortly after, however, he won the Baron de Forest prize awarded to the first Englishman to fly across the English Channel in a English-built plane – Sopwith had flown from Dover to east Belgium, the longest flight at that time from the UK to the European continent.

He also set up a flying school and in 1912 formed Sopwith Aviation in a disused roller-skating rink in Kingston upon Thames. There his company built aeroplanes, many of which saw action in the First World War. None was more revered or effective than the legendary Sopwith Camel.

A later collaboration with Harry Hawker led to the Hawker Engineering company, the forerunner of Hawker Siddeley (in which Sopwith served as chairman), which famously produced the Hurricane and other military aircraft during the Second World War. Ever adventurous, Sopwith also turned to yachting and led challenges for the America's Cup in

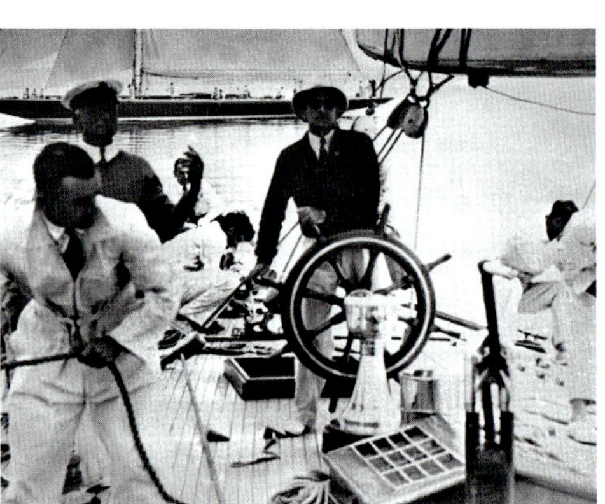

Right: Tommy Sopwith is pictured, at the age of 21, at the controls of his biplane in 1910 in which he flew across the English Channel

Below: Sopwith steers Endeavour II during his challenge for the America's Cup in 1937

CENTRAL

1934 and 1937. Sopwith was knighted in 1953. His last home was in Hampshire, where he lived until his death at the age of 101.

It was here in Green Street that Sopwith resided from 1934 until 1940, and his life is commemorated by a blue plaque placed by English Heritage in 1998.

Pioneering aviator and aircraft manufacturer, Tommy Sopwith also competed in the America's Cup

14

Sir Francis Chichester

1901 – 1972

9 St James's Place, St James's

SW1A 1PE

South Cloister, Westminster Abbey, Westminster

SW1P 3PA

Francis Chichester occupied rooms on the ground floor of this house in St James's Place for nearly 30 years. It was here that he planned his record-breaking solo circumnavigation of the world in the sailboat *Gipsy Moth IV*, completed in 1967. A blue plaque, placed in 1993 by Westminster City Council, records the home and base of this "Pioneer Aviator, Sailor and Author".

The son of a Devon clergyman, Chichester became a qualified pilot and was captivated by the challenge of long-distance solo air flights. During the Second World War, he used his skills to instruct and write about specialist navigation. After the war, he founded a successful map-making company. By 1960, Chichester had turned from aviation to long-distance yachting – winning the first Single-Handed Trans-Atlantic Race in a record 40 days, at the helm of *Gipsy Moth III*.

On 27 August 1966, Chichester set off from Plymouth in his 53ft ketch *Gipsy Moth IV*, returning to a hero's welcome on 28 May 1967 after 226 days of sailing with just one stop (in Sydney). By doing so, he became the first person to achieve a solo circumnavigation of the world. He was knighted in 1967. For

Right: Francis Chichester aboard Gipsy Moth IV prior to his solo circumnavigation of the world

Below: The Navigators' Memorial in Westminster Abbey

The courage and adventure of Francis Chichester thrilled a nation

the ceremony, Queen Elizabeth II used the sword previously used by Elizabeth I to knight Sir Francis Drake.

In the south cloister of Westminster Abbey, a colourful and artistic tribute known as the Navigators' Memorial was installed in 1979 and commemorates Sir Francis Chichester as one of Britain's great international sailors, alongside Captain James Cook and Drake.

15

Jack Broughton

1703 – 1789

West Cloister, Westminster Abbey, Westminster

SW1P 3PA

Staying in the sacred cloisters of Westminster Abbey, in the west cloister we surprisingly come across a leading prize-fighter of the 18th century.

Pugilism became one of the first sports to have a written code. Rudimentary rules were published by champion fighter Jack Broughton (*above, right*) in 1743 when he opened his own boxing amphitheatre. Broughton's 'rules' of how boxing should be conducted at his emporium essentially regulated the sport for a century or more, prior to the development of the Marquess of Queensberry's rules in the 1860s.

Becoming a respected figure in society, Broughton was appointed a Yeoman of the Guard at Westminster Abbey and it is here that he is buried alongside his wife. A gravestone, now sadly very worn and faint, can just be discerned on the floor of the west cloister. Originally, no reference was made to Broughton's fighting career. In 1988, however, the words, "Champion Prize-fighter of England" were inserted on the stone.

16

Sir Roger Bannister

1929 – 2018

Westminster Abbey, Westminster

SW1P 3PA

We stay in Westminster Abbey and pay tribute to the great Roger Bannister.

Could the mile be run in less than four minutes? It offered a tantalising symmetry – four laps, four minutes – and held an intense fascination for the sporting world. On 6 May 1954, Roger Bannister reached a new peak in sporting history. It was at the Iffley Road track in Oxford, just after 6pm, when the 25-year-old Bannister, a former Oxford man and now a medical student, turned to his colleagues, Chris Brasher and Chris Chataway, and said: "Yes. Let's do it."

Finishing with that long-legged, wide-striding run, face white and drawn, he burst through the tape totally exhausted. The chief timekeeper – 1924 100m Olympic gold medallist Harold Abrahams – handed the result to the announcer, who said, "The time was 3..." The rest was drowned in cheers and uproar. Yes, 3 minutes 59.4 seconds – the barrier had been broken. It was a defining moment in sport and a triumph that boosted the nation's post-war spirits.

Despite his professionalism in approach, this was also a triumph for the 'amateur'. Bannister would shortly resume a medical career in London and become a highly distinguished neurologist (*see also West London*). He was knighted in 1975.

In 2021, three years after his death, Roger Bannister's status in Britain's history was recognised by the installation of a Purbeck marble floorstone in the north aisle of the nave in Westminster Abbey with the commemoration: "Pioneering Neurologist, World Champion Runner".

Right: An exhausted Roger Bannister is surrounded by a joyous crowd after completing his epic sub-four-minute mile

Below: Stonemasons install the memorial in Westminster Abbey to honour Sir Roger Bannister in 2021

CENTRAL

A marble flagstone commemorates 'Pioneering Neurologist, World Champion Runner'

17

Olympic golden post box

Tothill Street, Westminster

SW1H 9LH

Golden 2012 champions celebrated around London include Andy Murray, Mo Farah and Natasha Baker

In Tothill Street, within sight of Westminster Abbey and Big Ben, a gold-painted post box – instead of the usual red – began the launch of Royal Mail's UK-wide programme of honouring each Team GB gold medallist at the London Olympic and Paralympic Games in 2012.

There are eight individual medallists (all featured in this book) for whom golden post boxes exist around Greater London. These are usually located in the areas where the individuals were born or grew up. In most cases, a basic explanatory plaque, including a braille version, has been added. Sadly, most of these are now worn and faint.

At first, the gold colouring was intended to be temporary but, in response to its popularity, Royal Mail declared that it would be retained. It added, however, that the programme was solely for London 2012 and not to be repeated for gold medallists at subsequent Games.

This post box does not commemorate any specific individual and has been painted gold to celebrate London itself as the host city of the 2012 Olympic and Paralympic Games.

Celebrating London as the host of the 2012 Olympic and Paralympic Games

18

Henry Mallin

1892 – 1969

105 Regency Street, Pimlico

SW1P 4EF

ENGLISH HERITAGE
HARRY MALLIN
1892-1969
Policeman and Olympic Boxing Champion in 1920 and 1924
lived and worked here

In Pimlico, we discover a plaque outside the former police training school at Peel House that celebrates Harry (formally 'Henry') Mallin – a fine middleweight boxer and Olympic champion.

Brought up in Hackney Wick, Mallin became a policeman. As a boxer, he was the Amateur Boxing Association middleweight champion for a record five years between 1919 and 1923. He triumphantly won the Olympic gold medal in Antwerp in 1920, outpointing the favourite from the US Army. Four years later, in Paris, Mallin became the first boxer to successfully defend an Olympic title in any weight division (remaining the only British boxer to do so until Nicola Adams repeated the feat in 2016). He never lost an amateur bout and never turned professional. A distinguished figure, he later managed the British boxing teams for the 1936 and 1952 Olympic Games.

In another historic first, in 1937 Mallin became Britain's first live television sports commentator, during a broadcast of an England versus Ireland amateur boxing match.

A blue plaque was erected by English Heritage at Peel House where Mallin was stationed from 1923 to 1931, including when he won his record-breaking second Olympic gold medal.

Harry Mallin was the first boxer to successfully defend an Olympic title

Above: Policeman and then-reigning Olympic boxing champion Henry Mallin poses at the Olympic Games in Paris in 1924

CENTRAL

19

Walter Wingfield

1833 – 1912

33 St George's Square, Pimlico

SW1V 2HX

Remaining in Pimlico, we find the former home of Major Walter Wingfield. Wingfield's invention and subsequent promotion of his court and equipment is regarded as the foundation of lawn tennis.

Large houses with gardens developed in England's rural suburbs in the second half of the 19th century, spurred in part by a surge in popularity for croquet. However, could a more energetic summer garden sport be devised to make further use of these lawns? Yes. In February 1874, Wingfield obtained a provisional patent for portable equipment for playing a game with rackets and vulcanised rubber balls that bounced on grass. The game was called 'Sphairistike' or 'lawn tennis', although the latter name was sensibly later fully adopted. *The Field* magazine, read throughout the shires, reproduced sections of Wingfield's booklet of rules which accompanied sets of equipment for his new game.

Major Walter Clopton Wingfield is celebrated as the 'Father of Lawn Tennis'

Lawn tennis swept through the English-speaking world. Others may claim to have developed or played similar games before him but it was Major Walter Wingfield who ushered the game towards its national, and later international, status.

Wingfield's court had an hourglass shape, with the net narrower than the baseline. It was The All England Croquet and Lawn Tennis Club (note the order) that introduced the first lawn tennis championship in 1877, adopting a rectangular court and other changes. The game became a major international competitive sport. A bronze bust of the Major can be found at the Wimbledon Lawn Tennis Museum (*see South-West London*).

His final home here in St George's Square bears a memorial plaque placed by the Greater London Council.

Former British Army officer Walter Wingfield poses with a racket for his new game

CENTRAL

Arthur Haygarth

1825 – 1903

88 Warwick Way, Pimlico

SW1V 1SB

Another Pimlico location returns us to the early days of cricket. Arthur Haygarth was a notable 19th-century amateur player who became one of cricket's most significant historians. He was the first sportsman to be celebrated under Westminster's green plaque scheme when a plaque was unveiled in 2003, exactly 100 years after his death here at his former home.

Haygarth played first-class cricket for the MCC and Sussex between 1844 and 1861, as well as playing for numerous other invitational and representative teams, including an England XI. Educated at Harrow, he served on many MCC committees. Haygarth was also a leading cricket writer and historian. He spent over 60 years compiling information and statistics, most notably his compilation: *Frederick Lillywhite's Cricket Scores and Biographies*, published in 15 volumes between 1862 and 1879.

In his *Wisden Cricketers' Almanack* obituary, Haygarth was described as "a famous cricketer, whose name will always be gratefully recalled as long as the game continues to be played".

Arthur Haygarth takes guard in one of cricket's earliest images

CENTRAL

"A famous cricketer whose name will always be gratefully recalled"

21

Lord Philip Noel-Baker

1889 – 1982

16 South Eaton Place, Belgravia

SW1W 9JA

Another fine sportsman who made a distinguished contribution to society following his athletic achievements was Philip Noel-Baker. He was a successful athlete who subsequently became a politician and Nobel Peace Prize winner.

Selected for the 1912 Olympic Games whilst at Cambridge University, Noel-Baker later became a silver medallist in the 1500 metres at the 1920 Olympics in Antwerp. After the First World War, he became a leading campaigner for the formation of the League of Nations and co-founder of the World Disarmament Campaign. Awarded the Nobel Peace Prize in 1959 and made a life peer, he was an active supporter of multilateral nuclear disarmament into the 1980s.

Noel-Baker lived and died here and is commemorated by a blue English Heritage plaque. A 'peace' garden in his name can also be found in Islington (*see North London*).

Philip Noel-Baker (extreme left) competes in the 1500 metres event at the 1912 Olympic Games in Stockholm

Philip Noel-Baker was an Olympic athlete and Nobel Peace Prize winner

CENTRAL

AAA
41

WEST LONDON

Roger Bannister trained in Paddington while a medical student and before his legendary sub-four-minute mile. Here in West London a plaque proudly celebrates this association. His feat remains a defining moment in sporting history.

WEST LONDON

In West London, we discover plaques and memorials recalling achievements from an eclectic range of sports and sporting eras.

In Paddington, we find the local training ground of two future champions in different sports born many years apart, as well as the grave of England's first football captain. In Chiswick and Hammersmith, we come across names that resonate in the history of British rowing. Statues in Chelsea and Fulham celebrate revered local footballing heroes. In Earls Court, two great sporting figures from the Commonwealth are remembered, and in the leafy suburb of Ealing we discover the homes of two outstanding British tennis players of the 20th century.

Wembley is a sporting cathedral where greats of sport have performed (in both the original and re-built stadium) and lifetime memories have been experienced – not only in football but also athletics, boxing and rugby league. Less expected, we come across the home of a pioneer of fitness training and a reminder of the 'fruit and veg' shop of one of Britain's most popular boxers.

1. **Sir Roger Bannister**
2. **Sir Bradley Wiggins**
3. **Cuthbert Ottaway**
4. **Olympic Games 1908**
5. **Howard Staunton**
6. **Eugen Sandow**
7. **Sir Learie Constantine**
8. **Arthur Stanley Wint**
9. **Joseph Bickley**
10. **James Hunt**
11. **Robert Coombes**
12. **John Wisden**
13. **Legends of Stamford Bridge:**
    Gus Mears, Peter Osgood, Frank Lampard
14. **Legends of Craven Cottage:**
    Johnny Haynes, George Cohen
15. **William Kinnear**
16. **Andy Holmes**
17. **Pete Reed**
18. **Jack Beresford**
19. **Dorothea Lambert Chambers**
20. **Fred Perry**
21. **Sir Arthur Elvin**
22. **Olympic Games 1948**
23. **Bobby Moore**
24. **Sir Alf Ramsey**
25. **Rugby League legends:**
    Martin Offiah, Eric Ashton, Gus Risman, Sir Billy Boston, Alex Murphy
26. **Lionesses of Wembley**
27. **Sir Henry Cooper**
28. **Natasha Baker**
29. **Chris Finnegan**

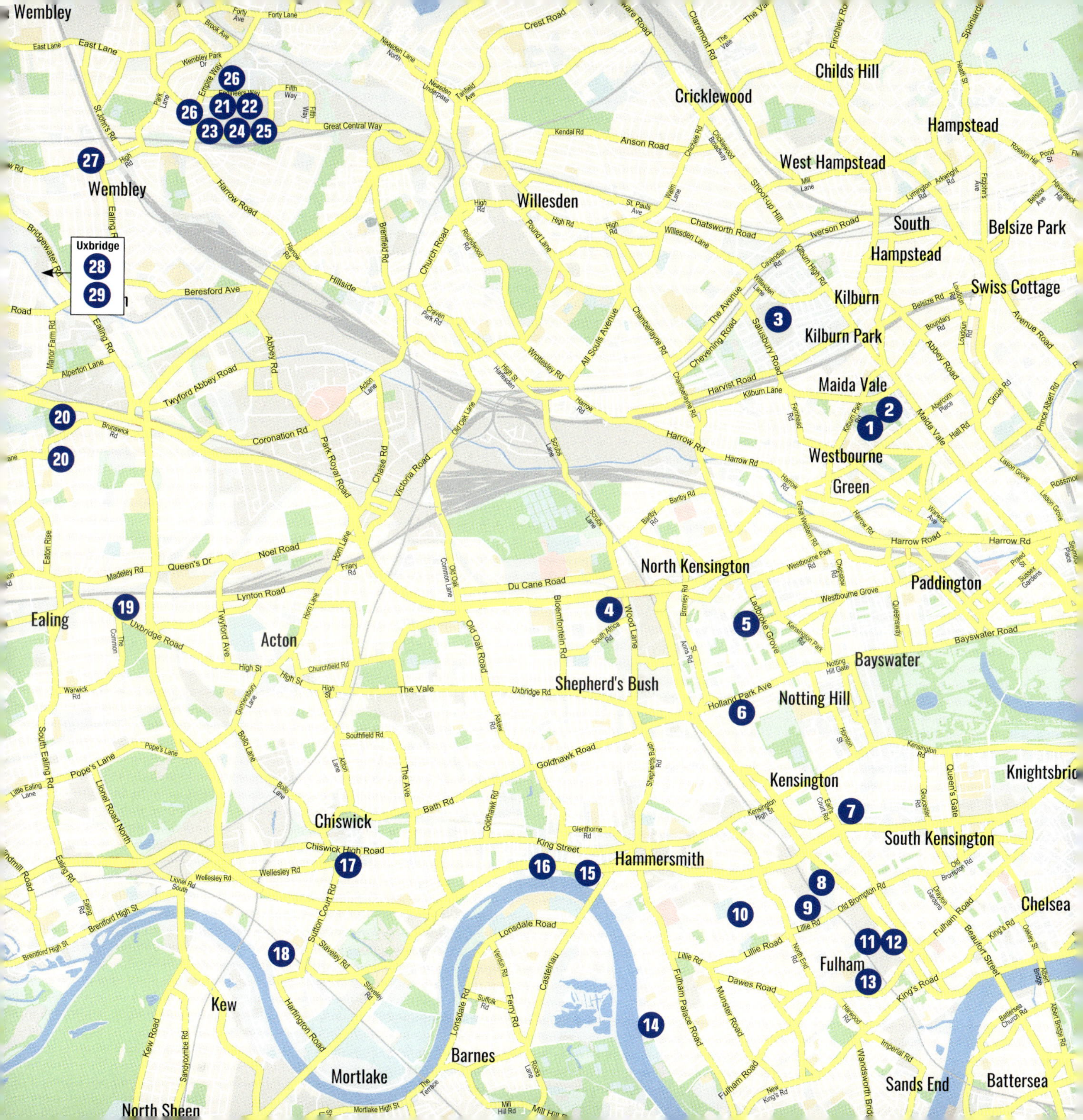

Wembley
Cricklewood
Childs Hill
Hampstead
West Hampstead
Willesden
South Hampstead
Belsize Park
Swiss Cottage
Kilburn
Kilburn Park
Maida Vale
Westbourne Green
Uxbridge
North Kensington
Paddington
Ealing
Acton
Shepherd's Bush
Bayswater
Notting Hill
Kensington
Knightsbridge
Chiswick
South Kensington
Hammersmith
Chelsea
Fulham
Kew
Mortlake
Barnes
North Sheen
Sands End
Battersea

1

Sir Roger Bannister

1929 – 2018

Paddington Recreation Ground, Randolph Avenue, Maida Vale

W9 1PD

We begin in Maida Vale where we enjoy another reminder of Roger Bannister. It was here at the Paddington Recreation Ground that Bannister trained for his historic sub-four-minute mile.

Born in Harrow, it was at Oxford University – where he was studying medicine at Exeter College – that Bannister started to take running seriously. He then became a full-time student at St Mary's Hospital Medical School in Paddington. Juggling his medical studies with running, he trained on the cinder track here "every day, between 12.30 and 1.30, then having a quick lunch before returning to hospital... we called ourselves the 'Paddington Lunchtime Club'."

On 6 May 1954, still in his final year as a medical student, Bannister completed his rounds at St Mary's, set off by train to Oxford and, with his colleagues and pace-setters Chris Brasher and Chris Chataway, waited for the wind to die down enough for him finally to challenge the sub-four-minute mile. History beckoned, and three minutes and 59.4 seconds later, it was made.

Bannister continued his medical career and became a world-leading neurologist. That moment in Britain's sporting history in May 1954, however, will always be for what he is most readily remembered. Two wall plaques at the front of the pavilion at the Paddington Recreation Ground, unveiled in 2000, recall his association with the site where the hard preparation for that historic run was undertaken.

The victory gasp that spells EFFORT
HANDSHAKES AND SMILES AFTER MIRACLE MILE
Daily Mail
DAILY EXPRESS
AT LAST—THE 4-MINUTE MILE
THIS IS IT—THE DREAM OF ATHLETES COMES TRUE . . . AND NOW, SOME BREATH
English victory beats world
DAILY SKETCH
DONE IT!
BANNISTER BEATS THE MILE
Seven Golden Daily Sketches
Daily Mirror
4-minute mile—it's OURS
NEWS CHRONICLE
BANNISTER BREAKS THE MILE BARRIER
DAILY HERALD
4-MINUTE MILE CRACKED BY ROGER

"We called ourselves the 'Paddington Lunchtime Club'"

Right: Roger Bannister is chaired by fellow medical students at St Mary's Hospital, Paddington, after his record-breaking run in 1954

Left: Newspapers hail Bannister's triumph in May 1954

WEST

MEDICAL SCHOOL

2

Sir Bradley Wiggins

1980 –

Paddington Recreation Ground, Randolph Avenue, Maida Vale

W9 1PD

We stay at the pavilion at the Paddington Recreation Ground to recall another great champion. Living nearby, it was here, on the former cycling track (removed in 1987) that a young Bradley Wiggins would first ride and aspire to become a racer.

Wiggins began his cycling career on the track with much success, winning gold medals at World Championships as well as successive Olympics from 2000 to 2008. He then turned his focus to road racing. Records and medals continued to be claimed. In 2012, he achieved the astonishing feat of winning the Tour de France, becoming the first British cyclist to do so, and in the same year winning the individual time trial at the London Olympics. Victory in the team pursuit in 2016 gave him a record-breaking gold medal at five successive Olympic Games.

Knighted in 2013, Wiggins retired from competition in 2016. In subsequent years, a doping controversy concerning Team Sky – for whom Wiggins rode from 2010 to 2015 – surfaced. Wiggins, however, has strongly and repeatedly refuted any allegations of doping on his part and has never been found guilty of any such infringement.

In 2013 a blue Bradley Wiggins plaque was erected here by the City of Westminster.

Bradley Wiggins, wearing the famous yellow jersey, heads for victory in the 2012 Tour de France

It was here that young Bradley Wiggins would first aspire to become a racer

WEST

3

Cuthbert Ottaway

1850 – 1878

Paddington Old Cemetery,
146 Willesden Lane, Kilburn

NW6 7SD

We move a few minutes north to Paddington Old Cemetery and discover a poignant reminder of the early days of organised football – now the world's most popular sport. Buried here is Cuthbert Ottaway, England's captain in the first truly representative international football match, Scotland vs England, which was played in 1872 in Partick, on the outskirts of Glasgow, and finished 0-0.

Schooled at Eton, Ottaway was a versatile sportsman. Captain of Oxford University's football team, who won the FA Cup in 1874, he was also a fine cricketer – opening the batting with WG Grace on many occasions in representative matches.

His grave, and story, remained neglected until recent years. Finally rediscovered in the north section of the cemetery, it was given a new memorial stone in August 2013 after a fundraising drive led by an England fan and supported by the Football Association (in its 150th anniversary year), the Professional Footballers' Association and the Old Etonian Association.

Cuthbert Ottaway was the first and led the trail for the likes of Bobby Moore and Harry Kane to follow.

Cuthbert Ottaway's grave and story remained neglected until recent years

Left: Cuthbert Ottaway's grave in Paddington Old Cemetery, which was renovated in 2013

Below left: A rare photograph of Ottaway, England's first football captain

WEST

4

Olympic Games 1908

White City Place, Wood Lane, White City

W12 7TP

London 1908 was the first modern Olympic Games to feature a purpose-built centrepiece stadium but, sadly, few remnants from the first Games to be held in England's capital city survive to this day. London had stepped in at short notice when Rome was unable to host the Games – funds reserved initially for the Olympics having been redirected following Mount Vesuvius's eruption in April 1906, which devastated the city of Naples.

The White City Stadium has long since been demolished, replaced by a cluster of offices comprising what is today known as White City Place. However, on the side of one of the buildings is a stone memorial to the 1908 Games, which was unveiled in 2005 on the centenary of the British Olympic Association.

Great Britain proudly found itself at the head of the 1908 medals table, but the most enduring hero of the whole Games was actually a disqualified foreign athlete. On the concourse in front of the 1908 memorial, the position of the stadium's athletic finishing line for the Olympics is marked. It conjures up the story of Italian marathon runner Dorando Pietri, who entered the stadium with a significant lead but began to stagger and promptly collapsed. Amidst a wall of noise, he was helped to his feet by a doctor and another official only to collapse again. As an American runner drew closer, Pietri was aided over the line in first place in front of the Royal Box to great cheering. He was later disqualified due to the assistance received, but it remains one of the iconic moments of Olympic history.

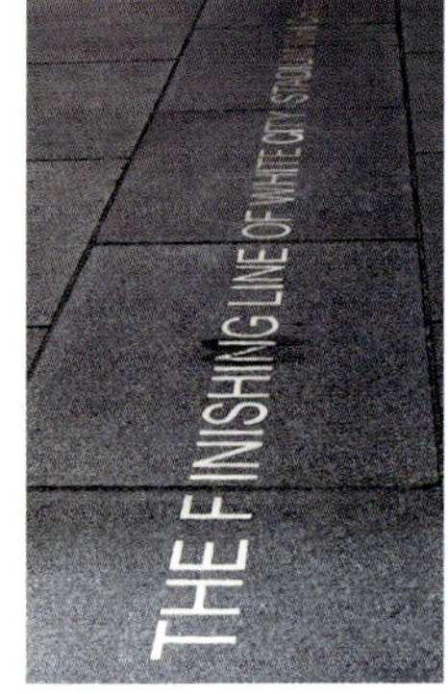

Above: The exact position of the Olympic finishing line in 1908 is marked in the paving stones

Right: Italy's Dorando Pietri is assisted over the line at the end of the marathon

WEST

The finish of the 1908 marathon remains one of the iconic moments of Olympic history

5

Howard Staunton

1810 – 1874

117 Lansdowne Road, Notting Hill

W11 2LF

We head south and make a stop in Notting Hill to admire a blue English Heritage plaque denoting the former home of Howard Staunton – regarded as the first and only British-born world chess champion.

Although an official world championship did not then exist, in the 1840s Staunton was widely regarded as the world's leading player after defeating the French master, Pierre de Saint-Amant. He is credited with helping to make chess a competitive activity. He was the principal organiser of the world's first international chess tournament – held in London in 1851 – and his writings were widely read and influential.

Commercially, he endorsed a set of distinctive chess pieces, which have become known as the 'Staunton Pattern' and are still accepted as the standard design for a tournament chess set.

We may debate the place of chess in the world of competitive sport but here in Notting Hill, where Staunton moved after living in Kensington, it is pleasing – if unexpected – to celebrate a British world champion.

Remembering the only British-born world chess champion

An artist's impression of a chess match between Britain's Howard Staunton (left) and Germany's Bernhard Horwitz in 1846

WEST

6

Eugen Sandow

1867 – 1925

161 Holland Park Avenue, Holland Park

W11 4UX

Born in Germany, Eugen Sandow was a well-known bodybuilder and showman. His fame helped popularise the practice of exercising for health and fitness. A blue plaque was unveiled by English Heritage outside the end-of-terrace house here in Holland Park where he lived from 1906 until his death in 1925.

Famous for his acts of strength, Sandow first appeared on a London stage in 1889. His celebrity was enhanced by studio photographs of the man known as 'the Father of Bodybuilding'. While living in London, he opened his own gymnasium, which he called the Institute of Physical Culture, in fashionable St James's. Here he taught methods of exercise, dietary habits and weight training as well as inventing various fitness devices, now familiar, such as rubber bands for stretching and dumbbells for strength building. He also promoted his fitness regimes and products. and even became a special physical instructor to King George V.

A bronze statuette of Sandow is presented to the winner of the Mr Olympia professional men's bodybuilding contest held annually in the USA. Here, in Holland Park, a plaque celebrates this "Body-Builder and Promoter of Physical Culture".

Strongman and showman Eugen Sandow lifts a weighty barbell in the late 1800s

A pioneer of bodybuilding and fitness training

7

Sir Learie Constantine

1901 – 1971

101 Lexham Gardens, Earls Court

W8 6JN

We move to Lexham Gardens in Earls Court and to the home for five years of Trinidad-born Learie Constantine. 'Connie', as he was affectionately known, was one of the great figures of West Indian cricket. He was the first outstanding black cricketer in English life and a pioneer who challenged the racial prejudices of the time.

A notable performance playing for the West Indies at Lord's in 1928 brought him to the cricketing world's attention. His attractive and attacking style – whether as a batsman, bowler or fielder – raised the profile of West Indian cricket. Connie became a professional in the Lancashire League for Nelson, where he was hugely popular. He captained the West Indies to their first series victory against England in 1934.

Outside cricket, he was a fighter for the cause of racial equality. He later became a barrister in Trinidad and then a government minister. Following Trinidad's independence in 1962, he served in London as High Commissioner of Trinidad and Tobago. Made a life peer in 1969, he was the first person of African descent to sit in the House of Lords.

Commemorated by a blue English Heritage plaque, 101 Lexham Gardens was his home from 1949 to 1954 and it was here that he wrote his most important book, *Colour Bar*, a critique of the racial discrimination he encountered in British life.

Below, left: Learie Constantine became a barrister and the first man of African descent to sit in the House of Lords

Right: 'Connie' walks out to bat past some enthusiastic young admirers in 1932

WEST

'Connie' was the first outstanding black cricketer in English life

8

Arthur Stanley Wint

1920 – 1992

22 Philbeach Gardens, Earls Court

SW5 9DY

Still in Earls Court, a plaque in Philbeach Gardens commemorates a standout victory in the 1948 Olympic Games in London, when Arthur Stanley Wint won the 400 metres and equalled the world record.

It was the first Olympic medal for Jamaica, not then fully independent of the United Kingdom, and *God Save The King* rang out around the White City Stadium. A member of Jamaica's 4x400 metres record-breaking relay-winning team in 1952, he also won a silver medal in the 800 metres in both the 1948 and 1952 Olympics. Wint is widely recognised as the inspiration behind Jamaica's rich athletic tradition. The country's Olympic legacy has since included such world-leading athletes as Donald Quarrie, Merlene Ottey, Veronica Campbell Brown, Deon Hemmings and, of course, sprinting superstar Usain Bolt.

Wint was also in active combat in the Second World War as a pilot with the Royal Air Force. Later a leading diplomat, he served as Jamaica's High Commissioner to the United Kingdom for many years. He remains a national hero in Jamaica.

Here in London, a wall plaque at the house where he lived for more than a decade was installed by the Nubian Jak Community Trust, celebrating the historic contribution of black and ethnic people in Britain and beyond.

Arthur Wint was the inspiration behind Jamaica's athletic tradition

Arthur Wint wins the 400 metres final in the 1948 Olympics

WEST

9

Joseph Bickley

1835 – 1923

62 Lillie Road, Fulham Broadway

SW6 1TN

Above a circular window at 62 Lillie Road, a royal crest catches the eye. This was the home of Joseph Bickley, a master builder whose name is still revered in the world of real tennis and rackets.

Based in Fulham, Bickley filed patents in 1889 and 1909 for a highly specialised plastering process enabling a 'non-sweat' wall and floor rendering that was perfect for the courts of real tennis and rackets – popular sports in many circles, particularly until the growth of lawn tennis. 'Bickley' courts were simply the best. More than a dozen Bickley real tennis courts around Britain and the USA are still in regular use, including two at The Queen's Club in Barons Court.

The royal crest? Bickley was a friend of royalty and rumours existed that the Prince of Wales (the future Edward VII) enjoyed trysts with actress Lillie Langtry in the studio at this house. More likely, however, the crest recognised Bickley's position as specialist supplier to the Royal household.

10

James Hunt

1947 – 1993

7 & 8 Normand Mews, Barons Court

W14 9RB

We move to a more modern age and a plaque recording one of Britain's most successful – and colourful – motor racing drivers. A plaque on the brick entrance to a gated mews house in Barons Court recalls that, for a period, it was the home of James Hunt.

Racing driver, and later broadcaster, Hunt was an exuberant character who led a swashbuckling life. Its peak was a triumphant victory in the Formula One world championship in 1976 – his first season in a McLaren car – by a single point over his great rival, the Austrian Niki Lauda.

After retiring from racing in 1979, Hunt established a career as a commentator and pundit for the BBC. He died, aged just 45, from a heart attack at his later home in Wimbledon.

11

Robert Coombes

1808 – 1860

Brompton Cemetery, Fulham Road, Chelsea

SW10 9UG

We move to Brompton Cemetery and dwell on a time in the early 19th century when the River Thames was bustling with constant activity and the sport of rowing flourished. In the south-east corner, near the Fulham Road entrance, a distinctive nine-foot-high tombstone resonates as a memorial to the glories of this age and the great rivalry between the watermen of the Thames and their northern counterparts of the River Tyne.

Robert Coombes led the London watermen. He became the champion sculler of the Thames in 1846 and held the title for six years, finally relinquishing it at the age of 43 to a man almost half his age. Not tall and weighing barely nine stone, Coombes' superior skill enabled him consistently to beat apparently stronger men. "The best-made men for rowing are those with good loins, wide at the hips, and long arms," he explained.

However, Coombes fell into poverty and ended up in a mental asylum in Maidstone, where he died, aged 52. The London watermen had not forgotten him, though, and friends and admirers funded his funeral and this distinctive monument. Carved in Portland stone, an upturned wherry boat rests on the top. Figures of watermen (for some years headless but now restored, two wearing the famous Doggett's Coat and Badge) can be seen guarding the four corners. One figure (Coombes perhaps?) holds a broken scull.

Despite weighing barely nine stone, Robert Coombes was the champion sculler of the Thames

Left: Historic Brompton Cemetery includes the resting places of Robert Coombes and John Wisden

Right: The striking tombstone of Coombes, 19th-century champion sculler of the Thames

12

John Wisden

1826 – 1884

Brompton Cemetery,
Old Brompton Road,
West Brompton

SW5 9JE

Amongst the notable figures buried in the historic Brompton Cemetery, in the north-east part of the graveyard we again come across a name synonymous with cricket.

We have already reflected on the career of John Wisden (*see Central London*) whose *Wisden Cricketers' Almanack* – first published in 1864 and the longest-running annual in sport – is known as 'the Bible of Cricket'. In 1984, on the centenary of Wisden's death, a headstone was placed at his previously unmarked grave in the cemetery. It recalls and commemorates one of cricket's most lasting names.

13

Legends of Stamford Bridge

Stamford Bridge, Fulham Road

SW6 1HS

Stamford Bridge is the home of Chelsea Football Club, and its grounds and museum recall the club's rich history (*see London's sporting museums & tours*). On the south side of the stadium, the brick wall at the back of the former terrace known as 'The Shed End' (a popular area for the club's die-hard standing supporters until it was demolished in 1994) displays images and descriptions of many of Chelsea's legendary players through the years, from Ray Wilkins and Ron Harris to John Terry, Frank Lampard and Didier Drogba.

Outside the stadium, a nine-feet-high statue, sculpted by Philip Jackson and unveiled in 2010, greets fans at the West Stand. **Peter Osgood** (1947–2006) was Chelsea's goal-scoring talisman. His skill, strength, eye for goal and confidence were much loved by the fans. Ossie died unexpectedly, aged 59, but the statue's 'King of Stamford Bridge' inscription still resonates with the club's fans.

Above: Peter Osgood stands in bronze, still 'King of Stamford Bridge'

Right: A sculpture re-enacts Chelsea founder Gus Mears' legendary dog bite story

WEST

Next, we recall the role of **Augustus 'Gus' Mears** (1873–1912) in the founding of the club. Originally an athletic ground, in 1896 Mears (*above*) and his brother Joseph purchased Stamford Bridge with a vision of creating the country's finest football stadium. But when nearby Fulham FC unexpectedly declined the chance to play there, Mears reluctantly agreed to sell the land to the Great Western Railway. He explained the situation as he strolled with his friend, Fred Parker, who still believed strongly in the football plan.

The story goes that Mears' dog, a Scottish terrier, leapt up and bit Parker's leg, drawing blood. Impressed that Parker stayed calm and laughed it off, Mears decided to accept his friend's opinion and declared he had changed his mind and would go ahead with the football scheme, even if it meant creating a new club. In March 1905, Chelsea FC was formed. A sculpture in the museum recalls the delightful story.

The dog bite that led to the founding of Chelsea FC

Legends of Stamford Bridge

SW6 1HS

continued

Above: The original wall of Chelsea's former Shed End, retained in part, honours the club's past legends

Right: A young fan 'meets' his hero

8
Frank
LAMPARD
Frank Lampard's stellar career is testament to the virtues of self-improvement and dedication.
Following his arrival from West Ham United in 2001, the young midfielder grew to become the club's most prolific goalscorer and central to our most successful period ever.
A record 164 consecutive Premier League appearances he set for an outfielder points to incredible consistency and resilience, but should not mask many other exceptional qualities.
Lampard played a vital role in Chelsea's remarkable run of trophy successes from 2005 to 2013. His were the goals which sealed the league title for the first time in half a century and he later added an FA Cup final winner at Wembley. He netted in our first Champions League final, was a supreme penalty taker and no one played more games in the league and cup campaigns that yielded the 2010 Double. Lampard jointly lifted European trophies with John Terry in 2012 and 2013, having led the team on the pitch in successive finals.
Renowned for his peerless ability to find space in the area - and then the net - Lampard eclipsed Bobby Tambling's long-standing Chelsea goalscoring record of 202 and left in 2014 having established a new high of 211.
Medals for three Premier League wins, four FA Cups, two League Cups, as well as those Europa League and Champions League triumphs, were rewards for hard work as well as physical and mental strength.
A three-time Chelsea Player of the Year, Lampard was named Football Writers' Footballer of the Year, runner-up in the 2005 European and World Player of the Year polls, and was routinely mentioned by his peers as one of the top exponents of the game.
His 13 years at the Bridge ensure he is one of the finest players in Chelsea's history, and many say the best of the lot.
Nationality
ENGLAND
Position
MIDFIELDER
Appearances
648
Goals
211
Che.lc/Lampard
LAMPARD
8

Legends of Craven Cottage

Craven Cottage, Stevenage Road, Fulham

SW6 6HH

We move on to Fulham's FC's Craven Cottage ground, where two local football legends are celebrated.

The first also serves as a reminder of a game-changing time when, in 1961, the campaign to abolish the maximum wage for footballers (then £20 per week) finally succeeded. Fulham's **Johnny Haynes** (1934–2005), was not only 'the Brylcreem Boy' (one of the first product endorsements by a footballer) but, significantly, became the game's first £100 per week player.

At Fulham, Haynes was 'the Maestro'. Renowned for his passing skills, he was a one-club man throughout his career. He led Fulham to promotion to the First Division

Haynes stands as if he'd just killed a lion in the jungle

Left: Johnny Haynes, maestro of Fulham, shows off his dribbling skills at Craven Cottage

Right: George Cohen, Fulham and 1966 England hero, stands proudly in bronze

during the 1958/59 season. He made 658 appearances for the club (594 in the league) and is still its second all-time leading goal-scorer and, with 56 international appearances for England (22 as captain), the club's most-capped player.

A splendid statue, sculpted by Douglas Jennings, was unveiled in 2008 and stands on a plinth outside the stadium. Haynes is in typical pose – hands on his hips, his foot on the ball as if, in the words of the statue's designer, "he'd just killed a lion in the jungle".

Where the Hammersmith End at Craven Cottage meets Riverside Terrace, another statue pays tribute to one of Fulham's finest. **George Cohen MBE** (1939–2022) was a classy right-back who played 37 times for England, including every minute of the glorious 1966 World Cup campaign. He also spent his entire career with Fulham and is celebrated with another statue by Douglas Jennings. Unveiled in 2016, the 50th anniversary of the World Cup win, it bears the inscription: "Fulham player. World Cup Winner. Gentleman."

15

William Kinnear

1880 – 1974

14 Lower Mall, Hammersmith

W6 9DJ

Above: William Kinnear, Olympic gold medallist in 1912, is commemorated beside the Thames at Hammersmith

The River Thames has played a central role in the history of British rowing, and in Lower Mall, near Hammersmith Bridge, a plaque denotes the site of one of the earliest amateur rowing clubs – the Kensington Rowing Club (now the Auriol Kensington Rowing Club) – and its illustrious former member and president, William Kinnear.

Kinnear was a Scot and an outstanding rower who won multiple championships on the famous river. He was champion sculler of the Thames from 1910 to 1912. Then, after rowing had become an Olympic event in 1908, he competed in the subsequent Games in Stockholm in 1912 where he comfortably won the gold medal in the single sculls. When the First World War broke out, he served with the Royal Navy Air Force and afterwards was a successful rowing coach.

Kinnear was subsequently a distinguished president of the Kensington Rowing Club and this riverside wall plaque – complete with the five Olympic rings – records his achievements.

William Kinnear was an outstanding rower and Olympic champion

Left: The stretch of the Thames between Putney and Chiswick, known as 'the Tideway', has a long history of rowing for pleasure, training and competition

WEST

16

Andy Holmes MBE

1959 – 2010

40 Upper Mall,
Hammersmith

W6 9TA

We stay with rowing and the Olympic theme but move into the modern era, albeit with a deep note of sadness. At the rear of Latymer Upper School, facing the Thames, a plaque remembers former pupil Andy Holmes.

Born in Uxbridge, Holmes was coached at the school and later, as a member of Kingston Rowing Club and the Leander Club, he became a great Olympian. Twice he rowed to gold medal success with Steve Redgrave – first in the coxed fours in the 1984 Games in Los Angeles and then again in the coxless pairs in Seoul in 1988. Holmes was also twice a World Rowing Championships winner.

He sadly died, aged 51, after contracting a serious bacterial infection.

Steve Redgrave and Andy Holmes (rear), gold medallists in the 1988 Olympics in Seoul

17

Pete Reed OBE

1981 –

Heathfield Terrace, Chiswick

W4 4JN

Nearby, outside Chiswick Town Hall, we come across a golden post box, one of a series painted by Royal Mail in honour of Britain's gold medallists at the London 2012 Olympics.

An officer in the Royal Navy and a mainstay of British rowing for a decade, Pete Reed is a three-time Olympic rowing gold medallist, including as a member of the winning men's coxless four at both Beijing 2008 and London 2012, as well as holder of multiple World Championship medals. Sadly, he suffered a paralysing spinal stroke in 2019. He is now a leading campaigner to improve the lives of wheelchair users.

WEST

18

Jack Beresford CBE

1899 – 1977

19 Grove Park Gardens, Chiswick

W4 3RY

In Grove Park Gardens, a leafy Chiswick street not far from the River Thames, we find the former home of one of rowing's legendary Olympians.

Born here in Chiswick and an amateur with the Thames Rowing Club, Jack Beresford was Britain's greatest rower during the period between the two world wars. Dedicated, disciplined and possessing a relentless will to win, he was Britain's most successful Olympian oarsman until the mighty Steve Redgrave more than a half-century later. Beresford won medals at five Olympic Games in succession from 1920 to 1936, a record since only tied by Redgrave. Olympic success included a silver medal in 1920 (single sculls) and gold medals in 1924 (single sculls), 1932 (coxless fours) and 1936 (double sculls).

Aged 37, he carried the flag for the British team at the opening ceremony of the notorious Berlin Olympic Games of 1936 and, with his colleague Dick Southwood, famously beat the German favourites for gold in the double sculls event – in front of a watching Adolf Hitler. It was his finest Olympic moment.

Beresford later became a successful coach and sports administrator and was a member of the organising committee of the 1948 London Olympic Games.

The name of Jack Beresford is still held in awe in rowing and the blue plaque erected here in 2005 was the first sporting plaque installed by English Heritage.

Right: Dick Southwood and Jack Beresford (right) are congratulated after their double sculls triumph in the Berlin Olympics 1936

Below: A 1932 diploma records another of Beresford's Olympic victories

WEST

In 1936 the British pair famously beat the German favourites in front of a watching Adolf Hitler

19

Dorothea Lambert Chambers

1878 – 1960

7 North Common Road, Ealing

W5 2QB

In a tree-lined avenue near Ealing Common, a plaque placed by English Heritage recalls Britain's most successful female tennis player in the period prior to the First World War – Dorothea Lambert Chambers.

Born Dorothea Douglass, she was the daughter of the vicar at nearby St Matthew's Church. It is said that she could constantly be seen or heard here using the walls of the vicarage – where she lived until her marriage in 1907 and which still stands today – for hitting practice.

She became a formidable champion, with a relentlessly accurate forehand, tactical skills and a steely determination. She won seven Wimbledon singles titles between 1903 and 1914 – a record only since bettered by two women and still by far a record for a British player.

Lawn tennis featured in early Olympics and she won the gold medal at the London Summer Games of 1908. Astonishingly, she continued after the end of the First World War and, aged 41, reached the Wimbledon final again in 1919, losing narrowly to the prodigious young Frenchwoman Suzanne Lenglen, more than 20 years her junior.

The plaque here in Ealing, erected in 2005, is a quiet reminder of one of Britain's great early champions.

She could be seen or heard here using the walls of the vicarage for hitting practice

Seven-time Wimbledon champion Dorothea Lambert Chambers was a formidable player

WEST

20

Fred Perry

1909 – 1995

223 Pitshanger Lane, Ealing

W5 1RG

The Brentham Club, 38a Meadvale Road, Ealing

W5 1NP

ENGLISH HERITAGE
FRED PERRY
1909-1995
Tennis Champion
lived here
1919-1935

EALING CIVIC SOCIETY
FRED PERRY
1909 - 1995
Tennis Champion
played here
1919-1935
THE BRENTHAM CLUB
THE BRENTHAM SOCIETY

We stay in Ealing to celebrate another tennis legend, Fred Perry.

Born in Stockport and having moved to Ealing aged nine, Perry was a table tennis champion before becoming the dominant individual lawn tennis player of his age. He led Britain to triumph in the Davis Cup for four successive years from 1933. In 1934 he won his first singles title at Wimbledon.

By the end of 1936 he had won three successive championship victories at Wimbledon, three in the US championships and one title each in France and Australia. He was also the first men's champion (there have only been nine) to gain a 'career grand slam' by winning all four major singles titles.

These were then firmly 'amateur' tournaments. Perry turned professional at the end of 1936, touring for many years, mostly in the USA where he fitted comfortably into the celebrity world.

Perry's formative years were in Ealing. It was here, at the family home in Pitshanger Lane, that he spent hours hitting ground strokes and volleys against the garage door and wall. At the nearby Brentham Club, the teenaged Perry won the club championship in 1926 and 1927. A plaque there was unveiled by the Ealing Civic Society in 2011. Nearby, a plaque erected in 2012 by English Heritage celebrates the home of Britain's great champion. After Perry, it would be another 77 years before a British male player would win the Wimbledon title.

Below: Fred Perry on his way to a third successive men's singles title at Wimbledon in 1936

Britain's finest men's tennis player of the 20th century

WEST

21

Sir Arthur Elvin

1899 – 1957

Wembley Stadium, Wembley

HA9 0WS

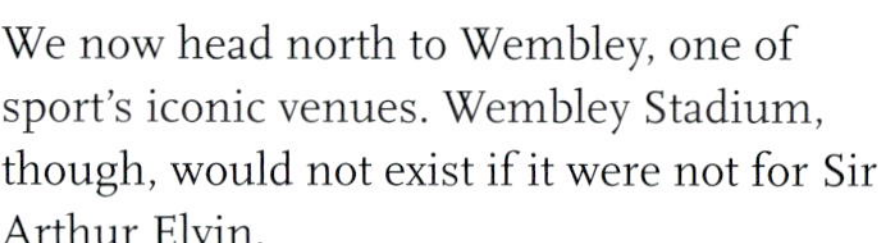

We now head north to Wembley, one of sport's iconic venues. Wembley Stadium, though, would not exist if it were not for Sir Arthur Elvin.

Initially built as the centrepiece for the British Empire Exhibition in 1924, the original stadium was afterwards little used except for each year's FA Cup final. By 1927, it was declared financially unviable and its demolition was planned. Elvin, a contractor who had once owned shops within the grounds of the exhibition, was engaged to clear the site. However, he saw the potential for the stadium to be the centre of a major sports centre and offered to buy it.

Despite nearly going bankrupt several times, Elvin eventually developed a viable business by introducing a variety of sports – starting with regular greyhound racing meetings, then others including speedway and boxing – to complement football. The stadium was saved.

Another pivotal moment was the London Olympics in 1948. Elvin made the site available, for free, for use as the principal Olympic stadium and Olympic Way was built. Elvin was later knighted for his services to the nation. The stadium was finally demolished in 2003 and the 'new' Wembley opened in 2007.

A bronze bust of Sir Arthur Elvin, by sculptor AJ Banks, was recovered from the royal tunnel in the original stadium and is now appropriately displayed in an entrance hall on the new site.

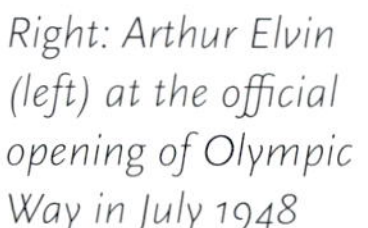

Right: Arthur Elvin (left) at the official opening of Olympic Way in July 1948

Below: Elvin inspects a model of new roads being built prior to the 1948 Olympics

Wembley was due for demolition but Elvin saw the potential and saved it

OLYMPIC WAY

Olympic Games 1948

Wembley Stadium, Wembley

HA9 0WS

London – having originally been selected to host the 1944 Olympics prior to the outbreak of the Second World War – was awarded the 1948 Games, and Wembley Stadium provided the setting for many key events, as well as a home for the Olympic flame

Today, at the modern stadium, only a handful of artefacts remain in acknowledgement of the venue's key role in this slice of sporting history. On an outside concourse, a concrete and tiled roll of honour saved from the exterior wall of the old stadium lists the 1948 gold medallists. Titles won by legends Emil Zatopek and Fanny Blankers-Koen particularly catch the eye.

Inside, a commemorative display cabinet includes a distinctive wooden shield from the 1948 Games. In a main entrance hall stands the original concrete pedestal and bowl in which the Olympic flame burned. Above it, a quote recalls Lord Burghley's stirring speech to a war-weary nation at the 1948 opening ceremony in which he welcomed "a warm flame of hope for a better understanding in the world which has burned so low".

Artefacts at the 'new' Wembley recall the original stadium's key role in the 1948 London Olympics

Wembley Stadium provided the setting for the Olympic flame

23

Bobby Moore

OBE

1941 – 1993

Wembley Stadium, Wembley

HA9 0WS

The image of England captain Bobby Moore raising the World Cup at Wembley in 1966 is one of the most enduring in football. Appropriately, a stunning, twice life-size statue of England's hero was commissioned by the Football Association from sculptor Philip Jackson for the opening of the new Wembley Stadium in 2007. Moore now looks down permanently upon Olympic Way with Caesar-like style. Around the plinth are representations of all members of that 1966 team.

Brought up in London's East End, Moore's promise was recognised early by West Ham. Soon made club captain, he was appointed England's skipper aged just 22. Manager Alf

Moore now looks down permanently upon Olympic Way with Caesar-like style

WEST

Ramsey called him: "My captain, my leader, my right-hand man." Moore earned a total of 108 England caps, 91 as captain. As a defender, his defining characteristic was his ability to read the play and anticipate the right move. He played his final professional game in England in 1978. He was sadly struck down by cancer and died aged just 51.

In addition to the imposing statue, as crowds make their way to the stadium along Olympic Way, the Bobby Moore Bridge reveals a set of tiled murals, unveiled by Moore's widow, honouring England's great captain.

Top: Alf Ramsey and Bobby Moore joyfully admire the Jules Rimet trophy in 1966

Above: Crowds now pass beneath the Bobby Moore Bridge on their way to the stadium

24

Sir Alf Ramsey

1920 – 1999

Wembley Stadium, Wembley

HA9 0WS

The architect of England's World Cup victory in 1966 was manager Alf Ramsey. Often inscrutable and unsmiling but with a firm and focused gaze, Ramsey was 'the General'. His famous exhortation to his players after West Germany equalised late in normal time during the final was duly followed: "You've won it once, now go out and do it again."

Ramsey had been appointed England manager in 1963 and was given full control to fashion the team in the style that he demanded. It was a major shift from the previous committee process of selection. If later years were less successful, he remains the only England manager to have won the World Cup. He was knighted in 1967.

Looking out from the players' tunnel at the new Wembley Stadium as the teams run out on to the pitch (or visitors tour the stadium), a bronze portrait statue of Ramsey (*above*) is raised on a plinth. He still holds that focused look of inscrutability.

Ramsey was 'the General'

Rugby league legends

Wembley Stadium, Wembley

HA9 0WS

Martin Offiah, Alex Murphy, Gus Risman, Billy Boston and Eric Ashton's widow are pictured at the unveiling in 2015 of the imposing statue at Wembley

Wembley is not only a mecca for football. It has also been the home of rugby league's Challenge Cup final since 1929, and a trip to Wembley is an annual pilgrimage for fans of the primarily northern sport. In 2015, when rugby league celebrated its 120th birthday, a 17-feet-high bronze statue by sculptor Stephen Winterburn was erected at the stadium.

It features five of the game's all-time greats. On his knees in celebration is **Martin 'Chariots' Offiah MBE** (1965–), who enjoyed four Challenge Cup victories with Wigan, one in 1994 featuring a stunning length-of-the-pitch try. Alongside him is **Eric Ashton MBE** (1935–2008), three-time Challenge Cup winner with Wigan. On high with the trophy is **Gus Risman** (1911–1994), who played an extraordinary 27 seasons and won three Challenge Cup victories, becoming its oldest-ever winner, aged 41, when leading Workington Town in 1952. Beside him is **Sir Billy Boston** (1934–), Wigan's record try-scorer, also a three-time Challenge Cup winner and one of the sport's most exciting and popular players. Completing the group is **Alex Murphy OBE** (1939–), the winning captain of three different teams at Wembley – St Helens, Leigh and Warrington.

The five players were selected by an extensive poll of stakeholders from across the sport. As Alex Murphy said at the unveiling: "A match at Wembley is the most important in a player's career... you always dream of playing at Wembley."

A trip to London is an annual pilgrimage for fans of rugby league

26

Lionesses of Wembley

Wembley Park Station, Bridge Road, Wembley

HA9 9AA

Wembley Hill Road, Wembley

HA9 0HB

Jubilation filled the air at Wembley on 31 July 2022 when a close-range extra-time goal from Chloe Kelly, London-born from Hanwell, secured a 2-1 victory for the England women's football team – known by all as 'the Lionesses' – against Germany to win the UEFA Women's Euro 2022 final. It was the first time since 1966 that any senior England football team had won a major competition.

The Lionesses had captured the nation's heart. For the final, the largest crowd in European international women's football history – 87,192 – was joined by a global TV audience of around 350 million. Distant was the ban imposed in 1921 on women playing football on pitches of clubs affiliated to the FA, which had stated that the game was "quite unsuitable for females and ought not to be encouraged". This ban was not lifted until 1970.

The Euro 2022 triumph has been celebrated around Wembley with a series of colourful murals from illustrator Nathan Evans, commissioned by Brent Council. They have been painted on three different railway bridges, with the two featured here being by Wembley Park station and the other near White Horse Square. The vibrant, naïve-style murals portray key expressions of individual players in the England squad.

The Lionesses' victory certainly acted as a booster rocket for women's sport. After reaching the World Cup final in 2023, their 2022 success was gloriously repeated at Euro 2025 with a dramatic penalty-shoot out win over Spain in the final in Basel. Two months later England's 'Red Roses' won the Women's Rugby World Cup for the first time since 2014.

Right: The Lionesses celebrate again at Wembley, this time in colourful murals (Top): Millie Bright proclaims victory, now before a local passer-by. (Bottom from left to right): Manager Sarina Wiegman and goalkeeper Mary Earps celebrate and Chloe Kelly acclaims her extra-time winning goal

Left: Leah Williamson (centre), England's captain, lifts the Euro 2022 trophy alongside her joyful teammates

WEST

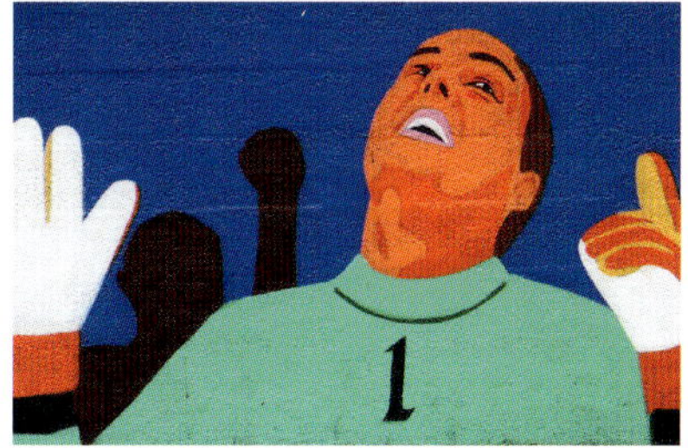

The Lionesses lit a booster rocket for women's sport

27

Sir Henry Cooper

1934 – 2011

4 Ealing Road, Wembley

HA0 4TL

No British boxer has been more popular and respected than Henry Cooper, many of whose fights were held at Wembley Stadium. Of these, none was more memorable than the famous night in June 1963 when ''Enry's' 'Ammer' floored a stunned Cassius Clay. Clay – later known as Muhammed Ali – was 'saved by the bell'.

Cooper, however, had another close association with Wembley. He lived here, with his wife and two sons, in Ledway Drive between 1960 and 1975. He was still at the top of his game as British and Commonwealth heavyweight champion but, now into his 30s, he was also planning his future. In November 1965 he opened his 'Henry Cooper – Fruiterer & Greengrocer' business in Ealing Road, near the junction with the High Road. Until its closure in 1968, the 'fruit and veg' shop was popular locally and passers-by often looked in to see if Cooper was inside, which he often was – the heavyweight champion happily chatting with customers.

Following a campaign by a local resident, a blue plaque commemorating Sir Henry's time serving the local community was erected in 2019.

Henry Cooper – boxing champion and Wembley greengrocer

Right: Heavyweight champion Henry Cooper welcomes customers at his greengrocers' shop in Wembley in 1965

Left: Cassius Clay is floored by 'Enry's 'Ammer at Wembley in 1963

WEST

28

Natasha Baker OBE

1989 –

High Street, Uxbridge

UB8 1JZ

We move further west to celebrate Uxbridge resident and outstanding Paralympic equestrian Natasha Baker. In the High Street, near colourful telephone boxes and the underground station, a gold-painted post box stands as part of Royal Mail's programme to honour gold medallists at London's 2012 Olympic Games.

Baker won two gold medals in 2012, and has since gained a further four gold medals in subsequent Games in 2016 and 2020. Her record has confirmed her place as one of Britain's finest Olympians.

The golden success of Paralympic equestrian Natasha Baker is celebrated (left) by Royal Mail in Uxbridge and (above) by the Freedom of the Borough of Hillingdon

Below, left: Baker celebrates winning gold at the London 2012 Paralympic Games

Born in Hammersmith, a childhood spinal illness left her with no feeling in her legs. She learnt to ride at a Riding for the Disabled Association centre and trains her horse to respond to her voice and saddle movements. A pavement plaque, located close to the 2012 post box and sadly in need of cleaning, records Baker's award of the Freedom of the Borough of Hillingdon.

Hillingdon's golden Paralympian

29

Chris Finnegan MBE

1944 – 2009

Hayes Amateur Boxing Club,
Judge Heath Lane, Hayes

UB3 2PF

Uxbridge was also the home of boxer Chris Finnegan, a locally born sometime bricklayer who was introduced to the sport by his brother at Hayes Amateur Boxing Club.

Finnegan became an Olympic middleweight champion, winning the gold medal in 1968 in Mexico City. A late addition to the British squad, southpaw Finnegan defeated the leading Soviet Union boxer in a close final contest. Wryly recalling his preparation for the high altitude of Mexico, he said: "I was up and down a 30-rung ladder all day with piles of bricks on both my shoulders. That was the only bloody altitude training I did." He memorably added: "I'm not just a silly old bricklayer now."

Turning professional, Finnegan captured the British, European and Commonwealth light heavyweight titles. He later became lifetime president here at the boxing club where it all started, which is also where a plaque proudly celebrates this boxing champion.

Chris Finnegan is welcomed back on his return to Britain after winning gold at the 1968 Olympics

"I'm not just a silly old bricklayer now"

NORTH LONDON

WG Grace, 'the Great Cricketer', dominated the cricket world for four decades. WG is a legendary figure at Lord's in North London where he is commemorated permanently in stone and bronze.

NORTH LONDON

North London is rich in sporting venues and heritage.

Undertaking a circular tour, we can sense the flow of sporting history: a famous pugilist of the 18th century; leading figures in the growth of organised cricket and the founding of the Marylebone Cricket Club; the first football captain of England; golf's first superstar; and the grounds of two world-renowned football clubs – one formed by a group of schoolboys and the other by munitions workers in London's East End.

We come across the homes of individuals who were pioneers in sport, from physical education for women and its inclusion in the school curriculum to the revolutionary design of motor racing cars, and – not least – trailblazers of women's participation in cricket and boxing. North London has also been home for Olympic champions and world leaders in athletics, cricket, golf, motor racing and boxing.

There is a deep and varied sporting heritage to be enjoyed in this distinguished part of the capital.

1. **Thomas Lord**
2. **WG Grace**
3. **More legends of Lord's:**
   Sir Pelham 'Plum' Warner, Sir George 'Gubby' Allen, William 'Bill' Edrich, Denis Compton
4. **Baroness Rachael Heyhoe Flint**
5. **Brian Johnston**
6. **William Lillywhite**
7. **Tom Sayers**
8. **Martina Bergman-Osterberg**
9. **Sir Learie Constantine**
10. **CB Fry**
11. **Harold Abrahams**
12. **Herbert Chapman**
13. **Gilbert Jessop**
14. **Graham Hill**
15. **Harry Vardon**
16. **The Walkers of Southgate**
17. **Charlotte Dujardin**
18. **Walter Tull**
19. **Legends of Tottenham Hotspur:**
    Bobby Buckle, Bill Nicholson, Ledley King, Harry Kane
20. **Nicola Adams**
21. **Colin Chapman**
22. **Laurie Cunningham**
23. **Legends of the Arsenal:**
    Herbert Chapman, Arsene Wenger, Tony Adams, Thierry Henry, Dennis Bergkamp, Ken Friar
24. **Lord Philip Noel-Baker**
25. **Gordon Signy**

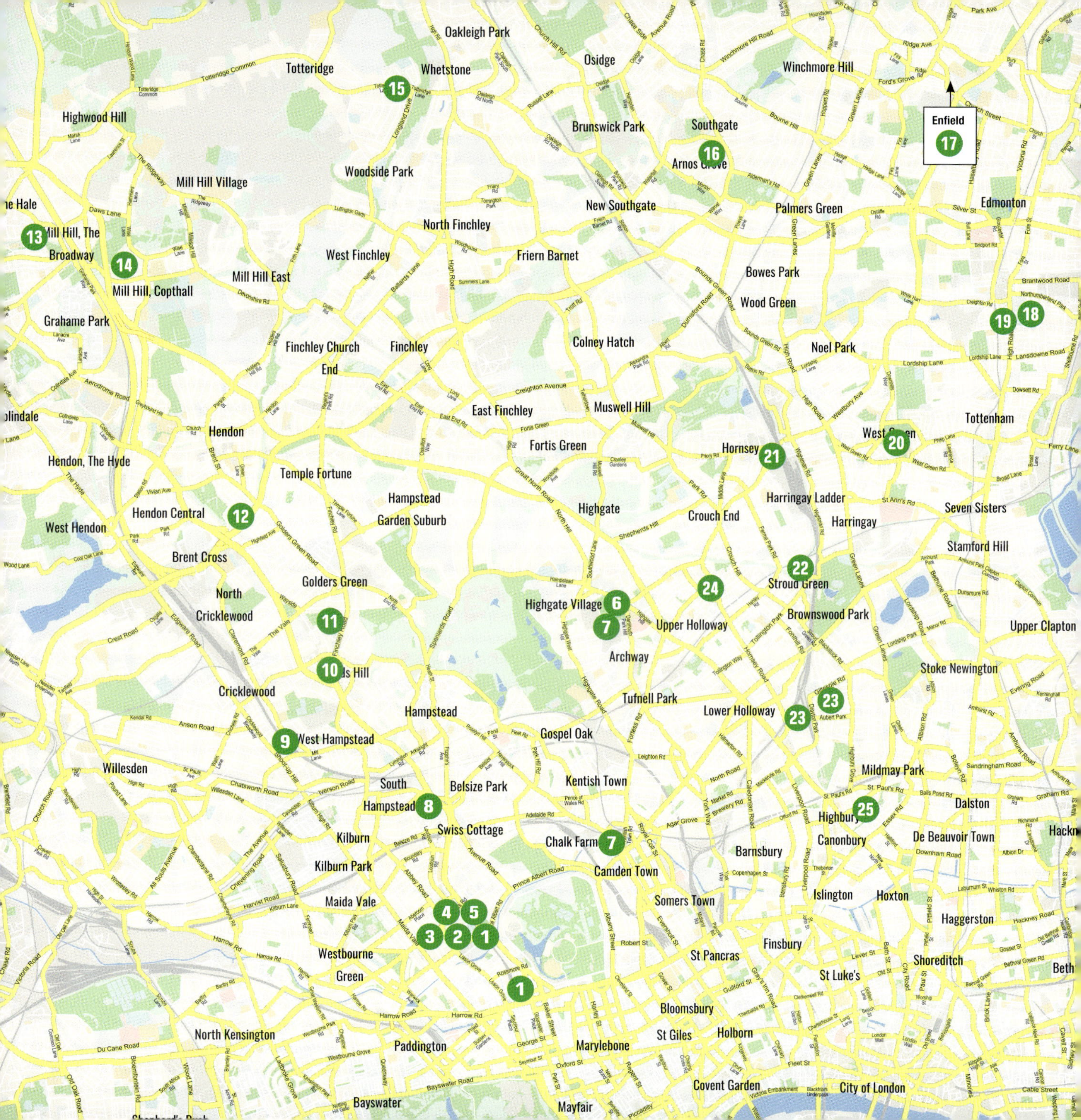
Oakleigh Park
Totteridge
Whetstone
Osidge
Winchmore Hill
Highwood Hill
Brunswick Park
Southgate
Enfield
17
15
16
Arnos Grove
Woodside Park
Mill Hill Village
New Southgate
Palmers Green
Edmonton
The Hale
13
Mill Hill, The Broadway
14
Mill Hill, Copthall
North Finchley
West Finchley
Friern Barnet
Mill Hill East
Bowes Park
Wood Green
Grahame Park
19
18
Finchley Church End
Finchley
Colney Hatch
Noel Park
Colindale
East Finchley
Muswell Hill
Tottenham
Hendon
West Green
20
Fortis Green
Hornsey
21
Hendon, The Hyde
Temple Fortune
Hampstead Garden Suburb
Highgate
Crouch End
Harringay Ladder
Harringay
Seven Sisters
Hendon Central
12
West Hendon
Brent Cross
Stamford Hill
22
Stroud Green
North Cricklewood
Golders Green
24
Highgate Village
6
7
Upper Holloway
Brownswood Park
Upper Clapton
11
Archway
Stoke Newington
10
Cricklewood
Tufnell Park
23
Lower Holloway
Hampstead
9
West Hampstead
Gospel Oak
Willesden
Mildmay Park
South Hampstead
8
Belsize Park
Kentish Town
Dalston
25
Highbury
Swiss Cottage
Kilburn
Canonbury
De Beauvoir Town
Chalk Farm
Kilburn Park
Barnsbury
Camden Town
Maida Vale
4
5
Somers Town
Islington
Hoxton
3
2
1
Haggerston
Westbourne Green
St Pancras
Finsbury
Shoreditch
St Luke's
Bloomsbury
North Kensington
St Giles
Holborn
Paddington
Marylebone
Covent Garden
City of London
Bayswater
Mayfair

1

Thomas Lord

1755 – 1832

Dorset Square, Marylebone

NW1 6PU

Wellington Place, St John's Wood

NW8 8QN

THOMAS LORD
laid out his original
CRICKET GROUND
on this site in 1787.
The M.C.C. was founded
here in the same year.

We begin in Marylebone and St John's Wood. This is a corner of London synonymous with cricket, and where the name of one man in particular has remained at the forefront of the sport for more than 235 years.

Born in Yorkshire, Thomas Lord was a general attendant at a fashionable sporting club that played cricket on the White Conduit Fields in Islington in the late 18th century. When the club members desired a more private venue, Lord – an ambitious, entrepreneurial fellow – was tasked with finding them a new ground. In 1787, he leased land in Dorset Fields on the Portman Estate and the club was reconstituted as the Mary-le-Bone Cricket Club (soon known simply as the MCC). Plaques on the green hut in the garden at (now) Dorset Square record the birth of the MCC and the first Lord's Cricket Ground.

In 1810, the lease came up for renewal and Lord chose instead to rent other fields nearby. This second 'middle' ground, however, was short-lived and required to make way for the Regent's Canal. Lord, having accepted compensation, identified alternative grounds in St John's Wood. The new location was a big success and the MCC became the most notable club in the land. Lord, aged 70, shrewdly sold the land in 1825 but the most famous cricket ground in the world continues to bear his name.

Above: A tiled portrait of Thomas Lord at St John's Wood underground station

Below: The founding of the MCC and the original site of Lord's Cricket Ground are recalled at Dorset Square

NORTH

An illustration depicts the colourful cricket and social scene at Lord's in 1822

On the corner of Wellington Road, unveiled in 1934, a listed stone bas-relief sculpted by Gilbert Bayes depicts a variety of sports, with cricket at the centre. It is headed proudly 'Lord's Cricket Ground'.

Less noticed, on the platform wall of St John's Wood underground station, a ceramic tile – one of many designed originally by Harold Stabler – quietly reveals a side portrait of Thomas Lord.

The most famous cricket ground in the world continues to bear Lord's name

2

WG Grace

1848 – 1915

Lord's Cricket Ground,
St John's Wood

NW8 8QN

William Gilbert Grace was 'the Great Cricketer'. The son of a family doctor near Bristol, he was initiated into the county and touring teams of the day through his father's contacts with the Duke of Beaufort. He would dominate the cricket scene for four decades.

WG's career statistics are incredible, with more than 54,000 first-class runs scored over an astonishing 44 seasons. He topped the first-class batting averages 10 times between 1868 and 1880. Still opening for England at the age of 50, he was said to be the best-known Englishman of his day. By the end of his career, the game had evolved and Test cricket had been established. "His bulk and stride carried cricket into the highways of our national life," proclaimed the doyen cricket writer Sir Neville Cardus.

After his death, the MCC constructed two sets of gates in his honour at the main entrance to Lord's (the WG Grace Memorial Gates). Officially opened in 1923, the cast-iron

NORTH

William Gilbert Grace was 'the Great Cricketer'

gates were designed by Sir Herbert Baker and bear motifs of a cricket ball and the sun's rays, as well as the initials of the MCC. Now Grade II listed, the gates are separated by a stone pillar topped by a carving of three stumps and an urn.

Grace is also represented in a life-size bronze statue, sculpted in 1999 by Louis Laumen in Australia, which was purchased by the MCC and placed in the grounds at Lord's. It depicts Grace in batting action in his later years – girth wider than in his early career, the cap too small by modern standards and that legendary beard exuding age and authority.

WG Grace bats in bronze near Thomas Lord's roller

3

Baroness Rachael Heyhoe Flint

1939 – 2017

Lord's Cricket Ground, St John's Wood

NW8 8QN

Rachael Heyhoe Flint in full flow for England in 1966

In addition to the main gate dedicated to WG Grace, another now honours Baroness Rachael Heyhoe Flint.

The face and voice of women's cricket for more than three decades, she was a true trailblazer. After her Test debut as a 21-year-old in 1960, she became England captain in 1966 and led her country, unbeaten, for the next 12 years. Significantly, she was a driving force behind the inaugural Women's Cricket World Cup, held in 1973, which England hosted and, propelled by her astute captaincy, won. Perhaps her most emotional moment came in 1976 when she led out England against Australia for the first women's match ever to be played at Lord's.

The MCC became central to her life. Her membership of the then all-male club was initially rejected. Having led the campaign for change, she was finally admitted when the MCC 'opened up' membership in 1999 – later becoming the first female on the MCC

A trailblazer, she was the face and voice of women's cricket for more than three decades

NORTH

Committee. She was also the first woman to be inducted into the ICC Cricket Hall of Fame.

After her death, the East Gate at Lord's was replaced in 2022 and renamed the 'Heyhoe Flint Gate'. Beside it, a fine bas-relief portrait sculpture by Robert Hunt was unveiled, with Heyhoe Flint bearing a well-deserved smile.

Heyhoe Flint leads out the England team in 1976 in the first women's match ever to be played at Lord's

4

More legends of Lord's

Lord's Cricket Ground, St John's Wood

NW8 8QN

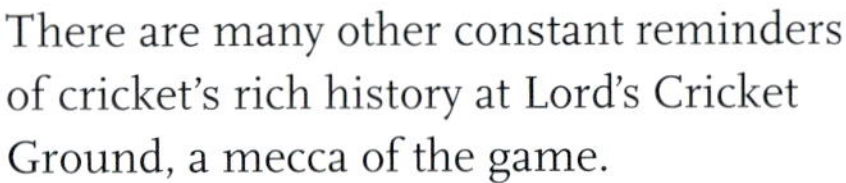

There are many other constant reminders of cricket's rich history at Lord's Cricket Ground, a mecca of the game.

The MCC Cricket Museum houses – in addition to the original Ashes urn – an unrivalled collection of art and memorabilia relating to the game's history and great players (*see London's sporting museums & tours*).

Four stands are named after distinguished figures from the ground's history. **Sir Pelham 'Plum' Warner** (1873–1963) was an England captain and MCC committee member, president and life-president whose connection with Lord's spanned almost 70 years. **Sir George 'Gubby' Allen** (1902–1989) also captained England and later became an administrator, including a tenure as chairman of the Test selectors for seven successful years from 1955. The twin stands at the Nursery End are named in honour of **William 'Bill' Edrich** (1916–1986) and **Denis Compton CBE** (1918–1997).

Edrich and Compton formed a supreme partnership – both for Middlesex and England – in the years after the Second World War. Edrich, convivial and party-loving off the pitch, was a steadfast pillar of English batting. Commentator John Arlott said of him: "[He] strides to the crease with the jaunty air of a man who has seen and solved it all before."

Denis Compton was his cricket 'twin'. Born in Hendon, he was a multi-sportsman,

Above: Pelham 'Plum' Warner (left) and George 'Gubby' Allen

Below: The Edrich and Compton Stands sit grandly astride the media centre at Lord's

NORTH

The MCC Cricket Museum houses – as well as the original Ashes urn – an unrivalled collection of art and memorabilia

playing football regularly for Arsenal in the winter. Renowned for his exciting style of play, he became one of England's most popular post-war cricketers. The glorious 'Summer of Summers' in 1947 saw him hit 18 centuries and record a batting average well into the 90s. *Wisden* proclaimed that "the exuberance of Compton's batting and personality became a symbol of national renewal".

Compton and Edrich are cheered off at The Oval in 1953 after a Test series win over Australia

Above: Bill Edrich and Denis Compton stride out to bat

5

Brian Johnston

CBE

1912 – 1994

Lord's Pavilion, St John's Wood

NW8 8QN

St John's Wood Church Grounds, Wellington Road, St John's Wood

NW8 7PF

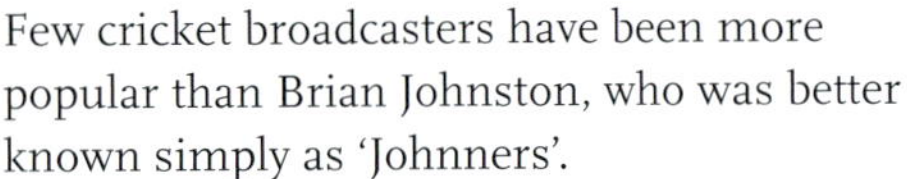

Few cricket broadcasters have been more popular than Brian Johnston, who was better known simply as 'Johnners'.

Johnston's popularity has led to two different and delightful memorials. A bas-relief portrait, sculpted by David Williams-Ellis and revealing that familiar smile, adorns a wall inside the Members' Pavilion at Lord's. Separately, in the nearby gardens of St John's Wood Church – well in sight of Lord's – the St John's Wood Society placed a plaque and tulip tree in 1994 in memory of their president.

Johnston was educated at Eton and Oxford (where he played a significant amount of cricket, perhaps a factor in his collecting a third-class degree). After the Second World War, in which he was awarded the Military Cross, he joined the BBC and later became a regular member of the television commentary team. Dropped from the TV team in 1970, he continued on radio's *Test Match Special* for another 22 years and became a national institution. His happy, ad-lib but knowledgeable style was a core feature of the broadcasts. After Johnston's death in 1994, Prime Minister John Major remarked: "Summer simply won't be the same without him."

Brian Johnston (above, left) smiles in bronze in the Members' Pavilion at Lord's and (below, left) is remembered as President of the St John's Wood Society

"Summer simply won't be the same without him"

6

William Lillywhite

1792 – 1854

Highgate West Cemetery,
Swains Lane, Highgate

N6 6PJ

We stay with cricket. In the north-east corner of Highgate West Cemetery, a notable sculptural tombstone – topped by a batting pad and decorative wreath – bears simply the worn inscription 'Lillywhite'. At the bottom, a stone carving displays a fascinating cricket motif – crossed bats and stumps with a ball removing a bail. This is a monument to William Lillywhite, an early 19th-century cricketer who helped transform the game.

Lillywhite was a successful bowler whose first-class career spanned nearly three decades. Importantly, he was a leading protagonist of roundarm bowling. Originally, all bowling was underarm, relying on spin and unpredictable pitches. However, by the early 19th century, the balance had swung firmly in favour of the batsman. Some bowlers – and Lillywhite was a lead exponent – countered this by bowling roundarm with the ball released from below shoulder height. This enabled more pace, 'cut' and bounce.

There was much controversy, but by 1835 the MCC had rewritten the laws of the game to permit shoulder-height deliveries, and by 1864 the bowler was allowed to do anything other than throw the ball. Many believe the game was saved by these changes.

The William Lillywhite monument, here where he was buried, was paid for by public subscription. Many of the Lillywhite dynasty would play significant roles in the history of cricket. No contribution to the game, though, was more significant than the change in bowling method of which William was a pioneer.

William Lillywhite was a game-changer in the history of cricket

A stone carving at the foot of William Lillywhite's tombstone in Highgate Cemetery

NORTH

7

Tom Sayers

1826 – 1865

257 Camden High Street, Camden Town

NW1 7BU

Highgate West Cemetery, Swains Lane, Highgate

N6 6PJ

Bare-knuckle prize-fighting had become clouded in illegality by the middle of the 19th century – with fights often broken up for breaching the peace – yet remained highly popular. Tom Sayers, known as the 'Napoleon of the Ring' due to his short stature, was widely recognised in this time as the heavyweight champion of England.

On 17 April 1860, a legendary fight – and one of the last major prize-fights in England – took place in Farnborough, Hampshire. Sayers, now 34 years old, fought America's champion John Heenan – taller, heavier and 10 years younger – for the unofficial 'World Championship'. The fight attracted enormous excitement and a large crowd from all strata of society. Heavy betting took place. The two fighters fought to a standstill for more than two hours across 37 rounds. By the end, Heenan was virtually blinded and Sayers had a broken arm. The makeshift ring-rope broke and an unruly riot began. The referee abandoned the scene and the fight was later declared a draw.

Sayers would, after retirement, be seen in the streets of Camden Town with his beloved bull mastiff, Lion. Weakened by alcohol and pneumonia, he died – aged just 39 – barely five years after that great fight.

A blue plaque, erected in Camden High Street by English Heritage, honours this sporting legend. Separately, a sandstone memorial tombstone (by sculptor Morton Edwards) stands towards the north-east

Tom Sayers on the ropes against John Heenan in the 37th round of one of the last major bare-knuckle fights in England in 1860

NORTH

corner of Highgate's West Cemetery. On the day of Sayers' funeral, thousands thronged the streets. Legend has it that Lion led the procession and later pined by his grave. Fittingly, a life-size cast of Lion rests at the foot of his master's tombstone.

Fittingly, a life-sized cast of Lion rests at the foot of his master's tombstone

8

Martina Bergman-Osterberg

1849 – 1915

1 Broadhurst Gardens, Hampstead

NW6 3QX

Martina Bergman-Osterberg was a pioneer of physical education for women and, consequently, women's sport. In South Hampstead, a blue plaque erected by English Heritage in Broadhurst Gardens in 1999 recalls this inspirational figure.

Born in Sweden and versed in the 'Swedish Drill' approach to physical education (PE), in 1881 she was employed by the London School Board and developed a course of instruction for teachers within the growing network of state-run schools. In 1885 she acquired the premises on the corner here at Broadhurst Gardens and established the Hampstead Physical Training College for women, the first of its kind. Subsequently moving to larger premises in Dartford, Kent, she inspired PE teaching as a new profession for women – and, importantly, the teaching of physical education as a subject in the school curriculum.

She also strongly encouraged women's participation in team sports for their health and wellbeing and was pivotal in the early development of netball as a sport. Her influence was far-reaching for generations. She would undoubtedly have relished the major advances in the popularity of women's sport in recent years.

She was a pioneer of physical education for women

Women exercise at Bergman-Osterberg's pioneering Physical Training College in 1938 after its move to Dartford

NORTH

9

Sir Learie Constantine

1901 – 1971

Kendal Court, Shoot Up Hill, Cricklewood

NW2 3PD

We move on to Shoot Up Hill in Cricklewood to recall again the inspirational story of Trinidad-born Sir Learie Constantine (*see West London*).

One of the great figures of West Indian cricket and, later, a leader and ambassador for the Afro-Caribbean community in London, Constantine in his later years lived here at Kendal Court. A wall plaque (erected by the Nubian Jak Community Trust in celebration of African and Caribbean history) commemorates this fighter for the cause of racial equality. Made a life peer in 1969, he became the first person of African descent to sit in the House of Lords.

10

CB Fry

1872 – 1956

8 Moreland Court, Lyndale Avenue, Cricklewood

NW2 2PJ

Charles Burgess ('CB') Fry was an astonishingly gifted all-round sportsman. A plaque at his birthplace in Croydon is featured elsewhere (*see South-East London*). Here, another – erected by the Hendon Corporation – marks the location of his home for the last six years of his extraordinary life.

Best known as a county and Test cricketer, Fry also played football for England, equalled the world record in the long jump and was a top-class sprinter and fine golfer – as well as being a diplomat, teacher and leading sports writer.

"He was probably the most variously gifted Englishman of any age," declared renowned cricket commentator John Arlott.

"He was probably the most variously gifted Englishman of any age"

NORTH

11

Harold Abrahams CBE

1899 – 1978

Hodford Lodge, Hodford Road, Golders Green

NW11 8NP

Echoes of *Chariots of Fire* and the 1924 Paris Olympic Games resound in Golders Green. Born in Bedford to a Polish-Jewish father, Harold Abrahams moved to London in around 1914 and lived here in Hodford Road during the time of his greatest success.

Educated at Repton School and Cambridge University, he was an all-round athlete – his feats including setting an English record for the long jump that stood for 32 years. First competing at the Olympics in 1920, with no success, he subsequently concentrated on sprint events under an intensive training programme led by professional coach Sam Mussabini.

Success came when Abrahams won the gold medal in the 100 metres at the 1924 Olympic Games in Paris, becoming the first European to win an Olympic sprint title. Running an Olympic record-equalling 10.6 seconds, Abrahams defeated his strongly favoured American rivals. The story became well known through the Oscar-winning film *Chariots of Fire*. Abrahams later captained the British athletics team in 1928 and went on to become a successful barrister, journalist and athletics administrator.

A plaque was placed at this house by English Heritage in 2007. Norris McWhirter, a leading athletics commentator, said Abrahams "managed by sheer force of personality and with very few allies to raise athletics from a minor to a major national sport".

Right: Harold Abrahams breaks the tape to win Olympic gold in the 100 metres in Paris in 1924

Left: Abrahams shortly after his golden triumph

NORTH

Abrahams' story became well known through the Oscar-winning film, *Chariots of Fire*

12

Herbert Chapman

1878 – 1934

6 Haslemere Avenue, Hendon

NW4 2PX

Born in a mining village near Sheffield, Herbert Chapman became a professional footballer with Northampton Town and it was there – as the club's stopgap player-manager – that his talent for management became clear. Moving to Huddersfield Town, he steered the club to two league titles and FA Cup success before leaving for then-struggling Arsenal in 1925. It was while living here in Hendon that this now legendary figure transformed the club.

Chapman also promoted many innovations to the game including rubber studs, player shirt numbers and floodlit matches. He introduced the Gunners' iconic red shirts with white sleeves and even persuaded London Transport to change the name of Gillespie Road underground station to Arsenal. More of his story is told elsewhere *(see page 124)*.

Chapman died suddenly in 1934 to the shock of the football world. In 2005, English Heritage erected here its first blue plaque for a person's contribution to football.

Herbert Chapman in his Highbury domain in 1932

Herbert Chapman transformed Arsenal and introduced many innovations to football

NORTH

13

Gilbert Jessop

1874 – 1955

3 Sunnydale Gardens, Mill Hill

NW7 3PD

Gilbert Jessop at the ready in 1903

Travelling south to Mill Hill, we turn to cricket at the beginning of the 20th century. A plaque, now largely hidden inside the porch of a semi-detached house in Sunnydale Gardens, recalls Gilbert Jessop who *Wisden* described as "the most remarkable hitter cricket has ever produced".

Jessop's scoring rate was unrivalled. Indeed (at least at the time of writing), he still holds the record for the fewest balls faced by an England player for a Test century – 76, in the fourth innings against a strong Australian side in 1902, a century that helped propel England to an improbable one-wicket victory.

Known as 'the Croucher' due to his stance, he made his debut for Gloucestershire aged 20 and firmly struck his first ball as a batsman for four. His many remarkable innings included 286 in less than three hours for Gloucestershire and 150 runs in an hour in a Test against the West Indies. He would surely have loved modern one-day cricket and 'Bazball'!

Jessop later moved with his Australian wife to London in 1924 and, as a good golfer, became secretary to a golf club in Middlesex. This plaque, erected by the Hendon Corporation at the house where he lived, recalls one of cricket's legendary players.

Jessop was "the most remarkable hitter cricket has ever produced"

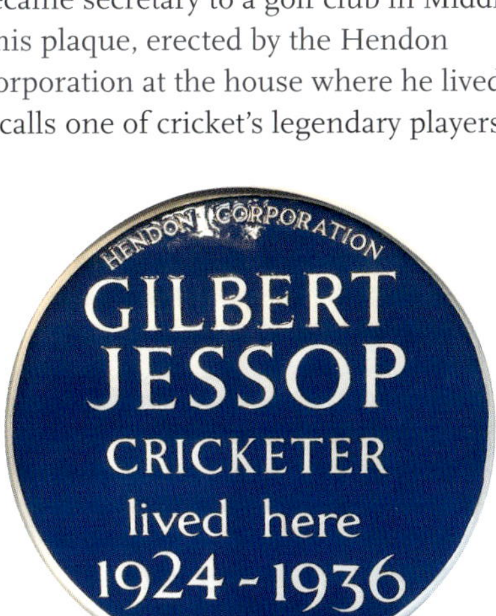

NORTH

14

Graham Hill OBE

1929 – 1975

32 Parkside, Mill Hill

NW7 2LH

Graham Hill, twice Formula One champion, before the German Grand Prix in 1972

Staying in Mill Hill, we remember motor racing champion Graham Hill. Hill was twice Formula One world champion and is still the only driver to have achieved motor racing's 'triple crown' of winning the Le Mans 24-hour race, the Indianapolis 500 and the Formula One title.

In 1962, driving for British Racing Motors, Hill won his first Grand Prix, and later that season, following a tense battle with Jim Clark, was named world champion – becoming the first British driver to achieve this success in an all-British car. A second championship followed in 1968, this time with Lotus.

Hill moved with his family to Mill Hill in 1960, and many of his triumphs were achieved whilst living here. It was also the childhood home of Hill's son, Damon, who himself became Formula One world champion in 1996. They are the only father and son both to win the title.

Moving later to Hertfordshire, Hill was tragically killed, aged 46, in a flying accident. It was Damon who, in 2003, unveiled the English Heritage plaque here at the former family home.

Graham Hill was the first British driver to win the Formula One title in an all-British car

NORTH

15

Harry Vardon

1870 – 1937

35 Totteridge Lane, Barnet

N20 0HD

Heading over to Barnet, at the corner of Totteridge Lane and Birley Road, we come across a plaque honouring a major player in the history of golf.

Harry Vardon took the sport to a new level. The power and accuracy of his shots were legendary. He won the first of his record six Open Championships in 1896 and was the leader of 'the Great Triumvirate' of British golf, alongside JH Taylor and James Braid. The trio dominated golf for two decades and did much to establish the game as an international sport.

Born in Jersey, after watching golfers on a nearby course Vardon quickly developed a talent for the game. He went to England and became a professional, working at various clubs before arriving in 1902 in Totteridge at the South Herts Golf Club. He remained the club's professional for 34 years. The club's main course is named the Vardon Course and a discrete statue inside the grounds celebrates its most famous professional.

A plaque recalling this golf superstar can be found at the home where Vardon lived during his many years in Hertfordshire.

Harry Vardon, in his 50s but still drawing the crowds at St Andrews in 1927

NORTH

Harry Vardon was golf's first superstar

16

The Walkers of Southgate

Southgate Beaumont
Care Community,
15 Cannon Hill, Old Southgate

N14 7DJ

In Southgate, a blue plaque at what is now a residential care home provides a glimpse of a remarkable story that began here, in the days before Test cricket, in the mid-19th century.

Four generations of the Walker family lived in the magnificent Arnos Grove House, which then stood in over 300 green acres. The family had a tradition of local philanthropy, and this included their major support of cricket and its growth in Middlesex.

A cricket ground was established by John Walker, the eldest of seven brothers, on the family estate. Teams would play, enjoy hospitality and later stay at Arnos Grove – with WG Grace and his brother, EM, visiting several times. Walker also founded the Southgate Cricket Club in 1855, which continues to prosper to this day. Many claimed 'the Walker Ground' to be the finest in the country.

In addition, brothers John, Teddy and

NORTH

There was an unbroken connection between the Walker family and Middlesex CCC for more than 70 years

Donnie Walker were among the founding members of the Middlesex County Cricket Club in 1864 and, when a county ground was needed, the Walker family were leaders and generous benefactors. In 1877, agreement was reached between Middlesex CCC and the MCC at Lord's, helping to set both on a sound financial basis in uncertain times. There would be an unbroken connection between the Walker family and Middlesex CCC for over 70 years.

At the site of Arnos Grove House, a blue plaque commemorates the Walker family's important contribution to the growth of cricket in Middlesex and London.

Left: The fine setting of the Walker Ground in Southgate during a Middlesex county game in 2006

Below, left: An engraved drawing captures Arnos Grove House in the early 1880s

17

Charlotte Dujardin CBE

1985 –

Colman Parade, Southbury Road, Enfield

EN1 1YY

In Enfield we recall the success of Charlotte Dujardin. Dujardin has been the dominant equestrian dressage rider of her era, with six Olympic gold individual and team medals, including three at the London 2012 Games – an achievement recognised by this gold-painted post box as part of Royal Mail's celebration of Britain's 2012 gold medallists.

Again a triple gold medallist at the 2016 Olympics, Dujardin has held all the world's elite dressage titles. Her recent career has been tarnished somewhat by a one-year suspension for excessive 'whipping' during training. She remains, however, one of Britain's most successful female Olympians.

18

Walter Tull

1888 – 1918

77 Northumberland Park,
Trulock Road, Tottenham

N17 0TH

In Northumberland Park in Tottenham, near the Tottenham Hotspur Stadium, a plaque – erected in 2014 by the Nubian Jak Community Trust celebrating the historic contribution of black and minority ethnic people in Britain – recalls the story of Walter Tull.

Born in Folkestone of a Kent mother and a father originally from Barbados whose own parents had been born into plantation slavery, Tull was brought up in a local Methodist orphanage after the early deaths of his parents. As a footballer, he was a member of Clapton FC's winning FA Amateur Cup team (*see East London*) before signing as a professional with Spurs and becoming, in 1909, one of the first black footballers to play in the First Division of the Football League. A centre or inside forward, there were several early reports of his skill. At many matches, though, he encountered racial abuse. In 1911 he was transferred to Northampton Town of the Southern League.

With the arrival of the First World War, Tull enlisted and served in the 17th Battalion of the Middlesex Regiment, the 'Footballers' Battalion'. He saw action on the Somme. Later, commissioned as an officer, he returned to the front as Second Lieutenant and was one of the British Army's first black infantry officers to lead troops into combat. He was praised in despatches for his "gallantry and coolness" under fire. In March 1918, in France, whilst fighting a last, desperate German attack, he was shot and killed in action.

Here, at 77 Northumberland Park, the plaque commemorates Tull at the house where the Tottenham Hotspur forward lived before the First World War.

One of the first black footballers to play in the First Division

Above: Second Lieutenant Walter Tull, pictured in 1917

Left: Tull the footballer poses at White Hart Lane, the home of Tottenham Hotspur Football Club, in 1910

19

Legends of Tottenham Hotspur

782 High Road, Tottenham

N17 0BX

We arrive at Tottenham Hotspur Football Club. Formed by young members of the Hotspur Cricket Club in 1882 so that they had a sport to play during the winter months, the name 'Hotspur' is thought to derive from a famous 14th-century knight, Sir Henry Percy, whose estate was nearby. Nicknamed 'Hotspur', he inspired the character of Harry Hotspur in Shakespeare's *Henry IV*.

A Heritage Trail now highlights features of the club's history (*see London's sporting museums & tours*). We dwell here on several significant figures.

Bobby Buckle (1868–1959), born and living just off nearby White Hart Lane, was – aged just 13 – one of the original founders of the club and became its first captain, with his home serving as the first registered address of the club.

Today, the club's Heritage Trail includes an old-fashioned lamp post on Tottenham High Road, symbolising the gas lantern underneath which – as legend has it – Buckle and his two school friends decided to form the football club, the lamp providing the light to enable them to take notes. A pavement plaque explains the significance of the site. Attached to the lamp post is the beautifully restored Cockerel Clock that previously resided outside the club's original White Hart Lane stadium.

Below: A lamp post on Tottenham High Road represents where legend has it the club was formed by young Bobby Buckle (above in later life) with his friends

The historic links are strong at Tottenham Hotspur

NORTH

In 1961, Spurs became the first team in the 20th century to achieve the 'Double' of winning the League Championship and the FA Cup in the same season. This was followed by victories in the 1962 FA Cup and, in 1963, the European Cup Winners' Cup – making Spurs the first British club side to win a leading European competition. The driving force behind this success and the team's attractive style of play was the club's legendary manager, **Bill Nicholson** (1919–2004).

Named the Bill Nicholson Gates, the black and gold iron gates which formed the entrance to the club's original White Hart Lane stadium – at which Nicholson was once memorably photographed – have now been restored and installed close to the new ground in honour of the club's great manager.

The original Bill Nicholson Gates have been cleverly incorporated into a famous photograph

19

Legends of Tottenham Hotspur

N17 0BX

continued

A powerful mural of Spurs legend Ledley King

Street art near the Tottenham Hotspur Stadium celebrates two legendary former players. One painted mural, commissioned by the Tottenham Hotspur Supporters' Trust, pays tribute to defender and captain **Ledley King** (1980–) and his well-known quote: "This is my club, my one and only club." King played 268 matches for Spurs and 21 times for England despite suffering from chronic knee problems for much of his career.

Another captures **Harry Kane** (1993–), born in Walthamstow (*see also East London*) and regarded as one of the club's greatest players. This vibrant mural on Whitehall Street, created by MurWalls, commemorates the moment the club's No.10 became its all-time highest scorer, surpassing Jimmy Greaves's total of 266 goals – a record set more than 50 years previously. Kane went on to score a total of 280 goals before moving to Bayern Munich in 2024. This dramatic street art has become a landmark reminder of his status and impact at the club.

Local hero and the club's all-time top scorer, Harry Kane, is celebrated in another eye-catching mural

20

Nicola Adams OBE

1982 –

Downhills Park, West Green Road, Haringey

N17 6PE

By a bench at the southern end of Downhills Park, a steel statue – commissioned by the charity Sustrans along its walking and cycling network – celebrates Nicola Adams, who trained at the Haringey Boxing Club when living nearby in London.

Adams joyously won the gold medal in 2012 (*above, right*) to become the first female Olympic boxing champion after the sport was introduced into the Olympic programme. This was a watershed moment both in her career – as it catapulted her to national fame – and for female boxing in Britain. She subsequently successfully retained her Olympic title in Rio in 2016.

Born in Leeds, Adams started boxing at an after-school gym class. She won her first fight aged 13 and never looked back. As an amateur, she won the entire set of championships available to her – Olympic, Commonwealth and European Games titles as well as World and European championships. Turning professional, she won the World Boxing Organisation (WBO) flyweight world title before retiring from an eye injury, undefeated, in 2019.

Adams' infectious personality captured the appeal of the public, and she has become

Right: Adams is declared the winner of Olympic gold at the Rio 2016 Games

a strong and inspiring advocate for equality and inclusion. When receiving an MBE from Queen Elizabeth II in 2013, she delightfully recalled the Queen saying she had watched her fights. She later reflected: "Wow, I was trying to picture the Queen sat having a cup of tea and putting the boxing on the TV."

"I was trying to picture the Queen having a cup of tea and putting the boxing on the TV"

21

Colin Chapman CBE

1928 – 1982

7 Tottenham Lane, Hornsey

N8 9DJ

Immediately recognisable to motor racing aficionados of the 1960s and 70s, the moustachioed Colin Chapman was arguably the most influential innovator in the history of British motor racing.

With a degree in civil engineering and a background in the RAF, Chapman was convinced that aeronautical techniques could be applied to tracing cars. He formed his own company, Lotus Engineering, built his own car and entered the world of Formula One with extraordinary success. His revolutionary design innovations included a one-shell chassis; improved aerodynamics through the use of front and rear wings; the relocating of radiators to the sides; and reclining the driver's position to reduce drag.

On the track, Chapman found his perfect partner in Jim Clark. The talented young Scottish driver clinched his first world championship in the Lotus 25 in 1963, nearly retained it in 1964 and convincingly regained it in 1965. Clark was tragically killed – driving a Lotus – in 1968.

Chapman himself died suddenly of a heart attack, aged 54. A plaque in Hornsey commemorates the original site of the Lotus Engineering Company, which started in old stables behind the then Railway Hotel on Tottenham Lane.

Colin Chapman was arguably the most influential innovator in the history of British motor racing

Colin Chapman (right) and Jim Clark in discussion prior to the Dutch Grand Prix in 1962

NORTH

22

Laurie Cunningham

1956 – 1989

73 Lancaster Road, Stroud Green, Haringey

N4 4PL

A blue English Heritage plaque on an end-of-terrace house in Lancaster Road in Haringey celebrates Laurie Cunningham. One of Britain's first leading black footballers, Cunningham lived here for nearly 10 years with his Jamaican parents as he progressed to football stardom.

Starting as a youth player with nearby Arsenal, he made his professional debut with Leyton Orient near where, a fan favourite, he is celebrated in bronze (*see East London*). A dazzling winger with an eye for goal, he then joined First Division West Bromwich Albion with great success. Manager Ron Atkinson once declared that Cunningham (also an adept dancer) "could run on snow without leaving footprints".

Having already played for England's Under-21 team, he was selected in May 1979 for the senior Home International against Wales – becoming the first black player to represent England in a senior competitive international (Viv Anderson having played in a friendly match a few months earlier).

Cunningham later joined Real Madrid in another 'first' for a British player, but was sadly killed in a road accident outside Madrid in 1989, aged just 33. A pioneer, his early days are recalled here in Haringey.

"Cunningham could run on snow without leaving footprints"

Laurie Cunningham in England colours in 1978

NORTH

23

Legends of the Arsenal

Highbury Square, Highbury

N5 1FE

Emirates Stadium, Holloway

N7 7AJ

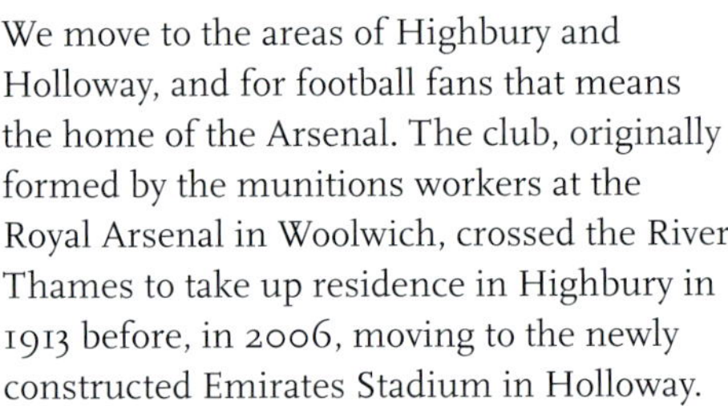

We move to the areas of Highbury and Holloway, and for football fans that means the home of the Arsenal. The club, originally formed by the munitions workers at the Royal Arsenal in Woolwich, crossed the River Thames to take up residence in Highbury in 1913 before, in 2006, moving to the newly constructed Emirates Stadium in Holloway.

Herbert Chapman (1878–1934) was the first major figure in Arsenal's history (*see also page 108*). Arriving at the struggling club from Huddersfield in 1925, he transformed the club. Arsenal won the FA Cup in 1930 and league titles followed in 1931 and 1933, becoming the first London side to win the First Division. He was the first manager to win the league title with two different clubs, having won it twice with Huddersfield. Shock was felt around the football world when he died aged 55 of pneumonia, just days after watching Arsenal's third-team match at Guildford while suffering from a chill.

The club, in tribute, commissioned a portrait bust from leading sculptor Sir Jacob Epstein. This can still be found in the famed marble entrance hall at Highbury, now the lobby for the new apartments that these days occupy the site of the famous old stadium. More recently, in 2011, a full-size statue was unveiled outside the Emirates Stadium as part of the club's 125th anniversary celebrations.

Below: The famous marble hall entrance at Highbury (now a residential development) is still home to the original bronze bust of Herbert Chapman

Herbert Chapman transformed Arsenal Football Club

NORTH

The Emirates Stadium is replete with memories from the club's history and tributes to its famous players

After Herbert Chapman, Arsenal's next great manager was **Arsene Wenger OBE** (1949–). The Frenchman was the first foreign manager to be an outstanding success in the top-flight of English football. Manager for 22 years from 1996, under his leadership Arsenal won the Premier League title three times and the FA Cup seven times – twice achieving the Double (in 1998 and 2002). In the 2003/04 season, his 'Invincibles' were undefeated throughout the 38-match league campaign.

Wenger's approach to player diet, scouting and training methods (including the use of science and data) changed the culture within the game. He was responsible for bringing foreign stars like Nicolas Anelka, Patrick Viera and Thierry Henry to England and later he led the club's relocation to the Emirates Stadium.

Now, since 2013, Wenger stands here in bronze (sculpted by Jim Guy) with club tie neatly in place, hands aloft, proudly holding the Premier League trophy.

23

Legends of the Arsenal

N7 7AJ

continued

The Emirates Stadium complex itself, ranging from the club's museum (*see London's sporting museum & tours*) to several surrounding statues, is replete with memories from the club's history and tributes to its famous players. Here, we dwell on some of the club's great figures.

Three statues were unveiled outside the stadium on the club's 125th anniversary in 2011. One was of **Hebert Chapman** (*see also pages 108 and 124*).

A second features **Tony Adams MBE** (1966–) celebrating his goal against Everton that clinched the Premier League title in 1998. Adams was first appointed captain in 1988 at the age of 21 by George Graham, and remained club captain for the next 14 years. He was the lynchpin of the Arsenal defence and is the only player to captain a title-winning team in three different decades.

Thierry Henry (1977–) was the third Arsenal legend to be immortalised in bronze in 2011. The Premier League became a magnet for great players around the world after its formation in 1992. Henry, a fan favourite and Arsenal's all-time leading goalscorer, was the first foreign star to be given this form of permanent recognition by the club. His memorable statue depicts him on his knees, acknowledging a glorious goal against local rivals Tottenham Hotspur in 2002.

Above: The peerless Thierry Henry on his knees in triumph

Left: Tony Adams' statue is a powerful reminder of a legendary Arsenal moment and player

Statues of club legends can be enjoyed around the stadium

23

Legends of the Arsenal

N7 7AJ

continued

Dennis Bergkamp (1969–) is the most recent Arsenal star to be celebrated in bronze outside the Emirates Stadium. A world-class player who was widely admired throughout the game, his 11-year career with Arsenal was filled with style, technique, physical strength and outstanding goals long-remembered by the club's fans. A dramatic statue, unveiled in 2014, depicts the Dutchman in flying action during a match against Newcastle in 2003.

We conclude with the statue of **Ken Friar OBE** (1934–). The story goes that, as a 12-year-old, Friar had been seen retrieving his football from under a car outside Highbury by Arsenal manager George Allison. Asked to report back the following morning, the boy was given a job running messages. Friar went on to serve the club for more than 60 years. In 2014, this delightful bronze statue was unveiled, capturing Friar playing as a boy.

The statues of Dennis Bergkamp (left) and Ken Friar (above) depict notable figures in the rich history of the Arsenal

24

Lord Philip Noel-Baker

1889 – 1982

Elthorne Park, Hazelville Road, Islington

N19 3NF

We have paid tribute earlier (*see Central London*) to the distinguished contribution to society of Philip Noel-Baker – the former Olympic 1500m silver medallist in 1920 who subsequently became an MP, co-founder of the World Disarmament Campaign, life peer and, notably, winner of the Nobel Peace Prize in 1959.

Here, within Elthorne Park, north of the Emirates Stadium, a quiet garden was opened in 1984 and dedicated to the memory of the peace campaigner. A plaque beside a gate to the garden reflects the dedication. A statue by Kevin Atherton, called 'Upon Reflection', was created as a celebration of peace and stands proudly in the garden.

25

Gordon Signy

1905 – 1972

23 Alwyne Road, Islington

N1 2HN

We end our circular tour of North London in Islington, where we come across the former home of a fine amateur sportsman who was also a pioneering medical doctor.

Gordon Signy was a lifetime fencing enthusiast. Although the Second World War deprived him of many years of likely international competition, he did captain the British fencing team at both the 1964 and 1968 Olympic Games. For some 20 years a leading member of the Amateur Fencing Association, he was a passionate proponent of the merits of the sport for young people.

Doctor Signy was, in addition, an eminent pathologist. He was a pioneer in the investigation and treatment of blood diseases, founding the speciality of haematology.

Signy is now commemorated at the home where he lived for 17 years by a plaque erected following a vote by the people of the Borough of Islington in recognition of this outstanding local figure.

EAST LONDON

Pride of East London – Bobby Moore raising the World Cup trophy in 1966 alongside England colleagues from West Ham United is an enduring image in sport and is celebrated in bronze.

EAST LONDON

East London has a long and proud history in many sports.

The East End – the area's historic core – was home to many leading pugilists, famous nationally in the 18th and 19th centuries, and this tradition has continued into the present day with a thriving community of boxing champions and supporters. In football, we discover the stories behind some of the world's oldest football clubs and, of course, East London was also the epicentre of the 2012 Olympic and Paralympic Games.

Notable sculptures on this circular tour of sporting heritage convey the pride of a community in the success of its local teams and sportsmen (and women) – not least West Ham's contribution to England's World Cup success in 1966. We also come across, often surprisingly, several sporting firsts, including the first Australian sports team to tour overseas; a boxer who became an Oscar-winning actor; one of the first black footballers to play in England at senior level; and the nation's oldest cycling club.

1. Jack 'Kid' Berg
2. Victor McLaglen
3. Daniel Mendoza
4. King Cole
5. Ledley King
6. Millwall Football Club
7. Teddy Baldock
8. Bradley Stone
9. World Cup champions
10 Legends of Upton Park:
Charlie Paynter, Billy Bonds, Sir Trevor Brooking
11. Bobby Moore
12. Barking & Dagenham sporting legends:
Bobby Moore, Sir Alf Ramsey, Jason Leonard, Beverley Gull
13. Ken Aston
14. Harry Kane
15. Beryl Swain
16. Leyton Orient Football Club
17. Laurie Cunningham
18. Pickwick Bicycle Club
19. Walter Tull
20. West Ham United's European champions:
Bobby Moore, Martin Peters, Sir Geoff Hurst
21. Olympic Games 2012

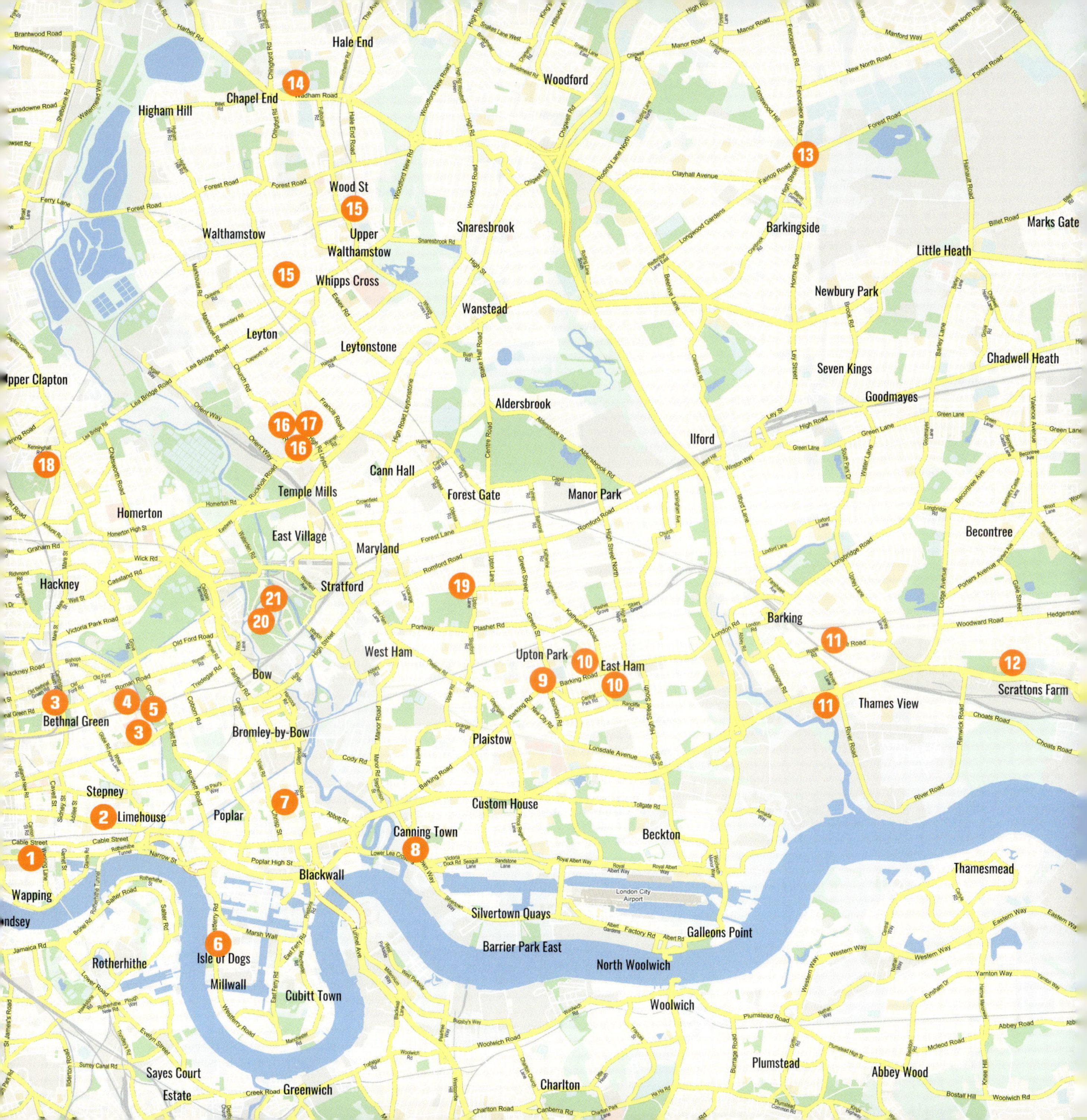

Hale End
Woodford
Chapel End
Higham Hill
Wood St
Upper Walthamstow
Walthamstow
Snaresbrook
Barkingside
Marks Gate
Little Heath
Whipps Cross
Wanstead
Newbury Park
Leyton
Leytonstone
Chadwell Heath
Seven Kings
Upper Clapton
Goodmayes
Aldersbrook
Ilford
Cann Hall
Temple Mills
Forest Gate
Manor Park
Homerton
East Village
Becontree
Maryland
Hackney
Stratford
Barking
West Ham
Upton Park
East Ham
Scrattons Farm
Bow
Thames View
Bethnal Green
Bromley-by-Bow
Plaistow
Stepney
Custom House
Limehouse
Poplar
Beckton
Canning Town
Blackwall
Thamesmead
Wapping
Silvertown Quays
Galleons Point
Barrier Park East
Isle of Dogs
North Woolwich
Rotherhithe
Millwall
Cubitt Town
Woolwich
Plumstead
Abbey Wood
Sayes Court Estate
Greenwich
Charlton
London City Airport
1
2
3
4
5
6
7
8
9
10
11
12
13
14
15
16
17
18
19
20
21

1

Jack 'Kid' Berg

1909 – 1991

Burlington Court, 88 Cable Street, Shadwell

E1 8GU

We start in the borough of Tower Hamlets where Jack 'Kid' Berg was one of many young Jewish men in the East End in the 1920s for whom boxing provided an escape from poverty.

Winning his first fight as a 14-year-old, he is said to have returned home with a black eye and to a scolding from his father until the boy pointed to the money won. His father promptly said: "Son – go back and fight again." Berg developed a non-stop punching style, attracting huge support and earning the nickname 'the Whitechapel Windmill' (after his place of birth). He later travelled to the USA and was a sensation. Handsome, charismatic and embracing the celebrity life, according to one commentator he "lived a furious life inside and out of the ring".

In 1930 Berg won the World Junior Welterweight Championship (to become the light-welterweight category) and four years later formally became British lightweight champion. Regarded as one of the world's best fighters of the era, he was inducted into the International Boxing Hall of Fame in 1994.

A memorial plaque, erected near Berg's childhood home by the Stepney Historical Trust, was lost when the housing estate was redeveloped but it has been replaced by this blue plaque on the wall at Burlington Court.

He lived a furious life inside and out of the ring

Jack 'Kid' Berg, the 'Whitechapel Windmill' and world champion in 1930

EAST

2

Victor McLaglen

1886 – 1959

505 Commercial Road, Stepney

E1 0HQ

Along Commercial Road we remember another boxer, albeit one who became better known as an Oscar-winning actor.

Born in Stepney, Victor McLaglen was brought up in South Africa and later went to Canada where his pugnacious character led him to become a professional boxer and local celebrity, touring with circuses and vaudeville shows. With the advent of the First World War, he returned to Britain and was commissioned into the 10th Battalion of the Middlesex Regiment.

McLaglen became heavyweight champion of the British Army in 1918 and, after the war, renewed his boxing career. He also, more notably, became an actor and a popular leading man in post-war silent films. Moving to Hollywood, he enjoyed many leading roles and earned an Oscar as Best Actor in the 1935 film *The Informer*, directed by John Ford.

A plaque on a three-storey house on Commercial Road, near Arbour Square Gardens, commemorates unusually this "Boxer & Oscar Winner".

Victor McLaglen (left) won an Oscar for this film, The Informer, in 1935

Victor McLaglen was both a heavyweight champion and Oscar winner

3

Daniel Mendoza

1764 – 1836

Tower Hamlets Environment Trust
Daniel Mendoza
Pugilist
1764-1836
English Champion who proudly billed himself as 'Mendoza the Jew', lived here when writing 'The Art of Boxing'.

3 Paradise Row, Bethnal Green

E2 9LE

Queen Mary University of London, Mile End Road, Mile End

E1 4NS

Continuing the East End's proud boxing history, we go back to the late 18th century when fights were rough, bare-knuckled and fought to a finish and prize-fighters were renowned sportsmen. Daniel Mendoza was perhaps the most famous of them all.

Brought up in Bethnal Green, he was a proud member of the growing Jewish community in London's East End. Known as 'Mendoza the Jew', his public fights attracted big crowds and much publicity. He enjoyed the patronage of the Prince of Wales and became recognised as champion of England. The most celebrated Jewish athlete of his time, his popularity was viewed as helping aid the integration of Jews in British society.

A pioneer in the ring, Mendoza also changed the sport through a more 'scientific' style of fighting, which included skilful side-stepping, fast-paced footwork and defence. He later set up a school to teach boxing and published the sport's first major instructional book, *The Art of Boxing*. Despite his success, Mendoza died in destitution.

A blue plaque, erected by Tower Hamlets Environment Trust, is attached to a terraced house in Paradise Row where he lived. He is also celebrated in bronze through a fine plaque by sculptor Louise Soloway (*right*), which was commissioned by the Jewish East End Celebration Society. The sculptural plaque was unveiled by Henry Cooper in 2008 at Queen Mary University in Mile End.

A colourful illustration of Daniel Mendoza's legendary fight against Richard Humphries in 1788

EAST

Prize-fighters were renowned sportsmen of the period and Mendoza was perhaps the most famous of them all

4

King Cole

c1838 – 1868

Meath Gardens, Smart Street,
Bethnal Green

E2 0SN

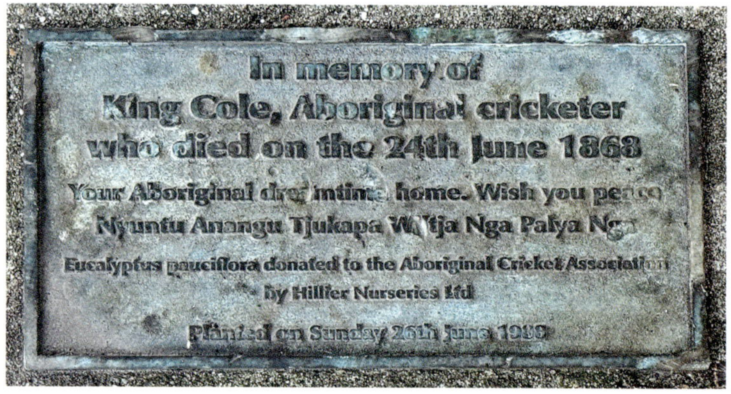

In Meath Gardens in Bethnal Green, a stone plaque in the ground beside a eucalyptus tree commemorates "King Cole, Aboriginal Cricketer". It is an extraordinary story from 1868.

There was no formal representative cricket in the mid-19th century, and teams and matches were organised by individuals. International sporting contact was rare and only three cricket teams (all English) had previously travelled abroad. Cricket had, though, also become popular in Australia and, in 1868, 13 Victoria-based Aboriginal cricketers were brought over as a team to England by an ex-pat, Charles Lawrence, amidst much curiosity regarding 'exotic races' from the colonies.

Nearly 10 years before the birth of Test cricket, this was the first-ever Australian sports team to tour overseas. Despite resistance from more conservative members within the cricket world, the touring team played many matches, including a narrow loss to the MCC at Lord's. The regally nicknamed 'King Cole' (whose real name was Bripumyarramin) was one of the team's best fielders. Sadly, he was taken ill after the Lord's match and later died, apparently of tuberculosis and pneumonia. He was buried in Victoria Park Cemetery, now Meath Gardens.

More than a century later, in 1988, the next indigenous Aboriginal side visited the UK as part of Australia's bicentennial celebrations. A plaque, as well as a eucalyptus tree, were installed by the Aboriginal Cricket Association in memory of King Cole and that extraordinary original tour.

Right: Aboriginal cricketers are pictured in 1868 during the first-ever overseas tour by an Australian sporting team

A stone plaque (above) set in the ground near a eucalyptus tree in Meath Gardens (below, left) marks the grave of cricketer 'King Cole'

King Cole and his Aboriginal compatriots were the first-ever Australian sports team to tour overseas

5

Ledley King

1980 –

Mile End Park, Bethnal Green

E3 5BE

By the canal towpath near Haverfield Road in Mile End Park, we come across an unusual and somewhat rusty silhouette statue of legendary Tottenham Hotspur defender Ledley King.

Born in Bow, King played for the local Tower Hamlets district team before joining Spurs, where he enjoyed a distinguished and highly popular club career as well as representing England. He is also celebrated in a vibrant mural near Spurs' ground (*see North London*) and features here, if abstractly, in steel near the area where he grew up. The statue was erected by the community organisation Sustrans as part of a series of 'portrait benches' on walking and cycling routes around England.

Ledley King was a 'one club' man and local legend

Spurs legend Ledley King is silhouetted, just, in steel

6

Millwall Football Club

Westferry Road, Isle of Dogs

E14 8LR

Here in the Isle of Dogs, on the pavement in Westferry Road near Cuba Street, we discover the origins of Millwall Football Club – or Millwall Rovers Football Club as it was originally called in 1885 – which was one of many clubs founded or encouraged in the Victorian era by local factories who believed sport developed character and a sense of community among the workforce. In the case of Millwall, the club was founded by workers from the local jam factory.

JT Morton, headquartered in Aberdeen, supplied sailing ships with food. It opened its first canning and processing plant (probably for more than just jam) in England at Millwall Dock, attracting a workforce both locally and from across the country. A football team was spawned, which played initially on local wasteland.

In 1889 'Rovers' was dropped from the name as, later, was its replacement 'Athletic'. After several different grounds, the club moved in 1910 to The Den in Bermondsey before leaving its intimidating ground there for the 'new' Den in 1993.

This simple stone plaque on Westferry Road is a delightful reminder of the origins of this distinctive east London football club.

Millwall Athletic FC in 1895, 10 years after the club's formation, when they were champions of the newly formed Southern League

The club was founded by workers from the local jam factory

EAST

7

Teddy Baldock

1907 – 1971

Langdon Park, Bright Street, Poplar

E14 0RT

We return to boxing and the sport's deep connection with London's East End. The story of Alfred 'Teddy' Baldock is one of a rise to glory followed by a sad and tragic decline.

Baldock, born and brought up in Poplar, was Britain's youngest boxing world champion. Fast on his feet and blessed with a strong punch, his lively style built a large following. In May 1927, aged 19, he fought the American Archie Bell at the Royal Albert Hall in front of an army of fervent supporters for the British Board's version of the then-vacant bantamweight world title. It was a momentous fight. Winning on points, Baldock became an international star.

Pride of Poplar – Teddy Baldock's story has been rediscovered but his statue sadly stolen

Although losing his world title four months later, he went on to win the British and Commonwealth bantamweight belts.

Sadly, his decline was fast. Burned out as a boxer by the age of 24, gambling, failed business ventures and over-generosity to so-called friends led to poverty and anonymity. He died penniless and forgotten in 1971.

His story has, though, been rediscovered. A fundraising campaign led to the commissioning of a fine bronze statue sculpted by Carl Payne. It was unveiled in 2014 in Langdon Park, close to Baldock's childhood home. Sadly, and criminally, in early 2026 thieves cut down and stole the bronze statue. The people of Poplar greatly miss a local hero and landmark.

Left: This statue of a local hero was supported by the Poplar Housing and Regeneration Community Association

Above: Teddy Baldock in training in 1929. A year later, he was Britain's youngest world champion

8

Bradley Stone

1970 – 1994

Peacock Gymnasium, Caxton Street North, Canning Town

E16 1JL

This statue in Canning Town is a reminder of an East End boxing tragedy.

The community Peacock Gym is well known for producing champion boxers and as a place for youngsters to develop and chase their dreams. Outside, there stands a statue of Bradley Stone, who died in 1994 aged just 23 fighting in a bout for the British super-bantamweight title. A fearsome left hook knocked Stone out in the 10th round. A few hours later, he fell into a coma and never recovered.

The statue of the young London boxer, sculpted by Ann Downey, was unveiled in 1995. The inscription acclaims: "A brave young man who died in pursuit of his dreams."

World Cup champions

Green Steet, Newham

E6 3DY

We move to the junction of Green Street and Barking Road, close to the site of West Ham's old ground near Upton Park. A magnificent 16-foot-high bronze statue by sculptor Philip Jackson celebrates England's 1966 World Cup triumph and the contribution of West Ham's golden trio – **Bobby Moore OBE** (1941–1993), **Martin Peters MBE** (1943–2019) and **Sir Geoff Hurst** (1941–). Commissioned by West Ham and Newham Council, it is simply inscribed: 'The Champions'.

The sculpture recalls the iconic moment when captain Moore was hoisted onto the shoulders of his teammates, with the final's hat-trick hero – Geoff Hurst – alongside. The only non-West Ham player of the four depicted, Ray Wilson, has his fist clenched. In the well-known photograph which inspired the work, Wilson's face was in a grimace (as he bore the weight of Moore on his shoulder) but the sculptor allowed himself one artistic licence and the Everton player now bears a smile.

The sculpture, unveiled in 2003, stands on circular steps on the main street. It remains here despite West Ham's subsequent move to Stratford. The names of the team and its manager, Sir Alf Ramsey, appear around the plinth. Nowadays, young children inspect the sculpture with curiosity while their grandfathers tell them of that day in 1966.

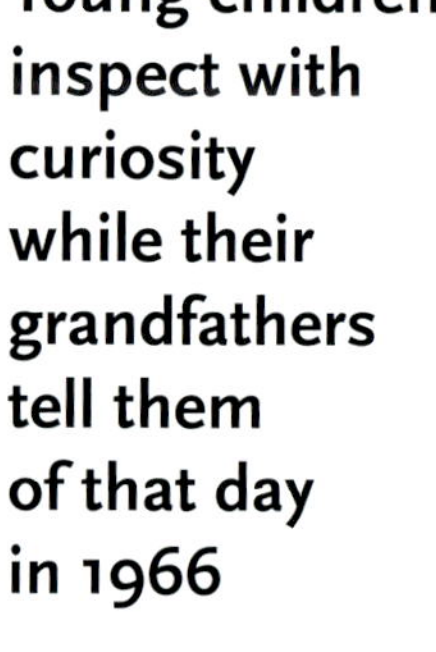

Young children inspect with curiosity while their grandfathers tell them of that day in 1966

England captain Bobby Moore, supported by his teammates, raises the Jules Rimet trophy in 1966

10

Legends of Upton Park

36 Ladysmith Avenue, Newham

E6 3AR

Priory Road, Newham

E6 1PU

Reminders of West Ham United's memorable days at its atmospheric former ground near Upton Park remain in the area despite the club's move to the London Stadium in 2013.

A plaque in Ladysmith Avenue recalls club legend **Charlie Paynter** (1879–1970). He began his career as an unpaid help at the club in 1897, when it was Thameside Ironworks FC (hence the crossed hammers badge and 'Hammers' nickname). His association with the club – which became West Ham United in 1900 – lasted for more than 70 years as player, trainer and then manager from 1932 until 1950. He introduced to the club a distinctive style and a 'family' tradition, as well as leading it to its first-ever FA Cup trophy in 1940. He was 'Mr West Ham'.

Upon his retirement as manager in 1950, a testimonial match was held in his honour, the first of its kind at the club. Appropriately, after the Second World War, one of the attendees was his next-door neighbour – and the 'Forces' sweetheart ' – Vera Lynn, who became a Dame in 1975.

In 2017, Newham Council, as part of its Heritage Project highlighting famous figures to have lived in Newham, erected a blue plaque here at Paynter's former home.

Charlie Paynter, 'Mr West Ham', is pictured in 1964. His association with the club began in 1897

EAST

Together, Bonds and Brooking symbolise the 'claret and blue'

A colourful painted mural in Priory Road, near to the old Upton Park ground, celebrates two local and long-serving playing legends of the club. **Billy Bonds MBE** (1946–2025), was born in Woolwich and made a record 799 West Ham appearances over 21 seasons from 1967. A defender admired for his energy, strength and competitive attitude, as well as his straggling hair, Bonds was a huge fan favourite. He captained the club to two FA Cup triumphs and also managed the Hammers for a period.

Alongside Bonds is **Sir Trevor Brooking** (1948–). Born in Barking, he also made his senior debut in 1967. An attacking midfielder of style and authority, he graced the club with 647 appearances, twice winning the FA Cup and earning 47 England caps. As an administrator, his roles have included chairman of Sport England and FA Director of Football Development. He was knighted in 2004.

Together, Bonds and Brooking symbolise the 'claret and blue'. Other club legends at the heart of England's 1966 World Cup success are also celebrated in these streets. West Ham fans are justly proud of their club's legacy.

Hammers legends Billy Bonds and Trevor Brooking have been brought together again in this vibrant mural near Upton Park

11

Bobby Moore OBE

1941 – 1993

43 Waverley Gardens, Barking

IG11 0BH

Ripple Primary School, Ripple Road, Barking

IG11 7QS

ENGLISH HERITAGE
BOBBY MOORE
1941 - 1993
Captain of the World Cup-winning England Football Team lived here

We divert a short distance to Barking to reflect on the childhood of Bobby Moore. No figure in West Ham's history is more revered than the legendary leader. Playing well over 600 games for the Hammers across 16 seasons – as captain for more than 10 of those – Moore is widely regarded as one of the game's greatest defenders.

A first Wembley triumph came in 1964 when he captained West Ham to FA Cup victory over Preston North End. The following year he led the club to success in the European Cup Winners' Cup. Then came England's 1966 World Cup triumph.

This local and national icon is celebrated in both bronze and plaque in several places

This local and national icon is celebrated in both bronze and plaque

EAST

Above: Bobby Moore's childhood home in Barking

Left: 18-year-old Moore, already a first-team player for West Ham

West Ham skipper Bobby Moore leads out his team at Upton Park in 1970

around London (*see also West London*). In 2008, 15 years after his untimely death, West Ham officially 'retired' the club's No.6 shirt in honour of its legendary player.

In Waverley Gardens, we celebrate Moore's early life. In 2016, a blue plaque was erected by English Heritage at Moore's childhood home. While living there, he attended Ripple Primary School where, at the Westbury Site, another plaque recalls the school's most famous pupil. The young Bobby Moore played football in kickabouts with his father and uncle in nearby Greatfields Park before commencing his career with West Ham, making his debut as a 17-year-old. A regal career followed.

12

Barking & Dagenham sporting legends

Gale Street, Dagenham

IG11 0TT

Beside the passing traffic on the A13, unusual metal sculptures feature the silhouette profiles of five sporting legends, all born in Barking or Dagenham. Reflecting the pride of a local community in their sporting success, the artwork was commissioned by the local council as part of the celebratory lead-up to the 2012 Olympic and Paralympic Games.

One features **Bobby Moore OBE**, born in Barking and England's 1966 World Cup captain. Alongside Moore is his international manager, **Sir Alf Ramsey**, born in Dagenham and knighted in 1967 in recognition of England's World Cup victory. **Jason Leonard OBE**, born in Barking, is England's most-capped rugby union player; a prop forward in the dominant pack during the team's highly successful period in the late 1990s and early 2000s, including the 2003 World Cup victory. **Beverley Gull MBE** contracted polio as a child and then suffered a car accident resulting in paraplegia. Swimming was part of her rehabilitation programme and swiftly became her passion. She went on to compete in her first Paralympics in Seoul in 1988 – winning three individual gold medals – and during her 11-year swimming career she won more than 40 international gold medals and broke 13 world records.

The sculptures are positioned on a grass mound off Gale Street – the very street in which Gull grew up.

Clockwise from top left: Bobby Moore, Alf Ramsey, Beverley Gull and Jason Leonard – all born nearby – are celebrated beside the A13

EAST

Remembering four locally born legends

RAMSEY
BOBBY MOORE
BEVERLEY GULL

13

Ken Aston MBE

1915 – 2001

Ken Aston Square,
140 High Street, Ilford

IG6 2EA

Distinguished football referee Ken Aston at the 1966 World Cup

This unlikely local hero is commemorated not only with a plaque but also has a town square named after him. Ken Aston was a renowned international football referee who was responsible for numerous innovations relating to the officiating of the game.

Brought up in Redbridge, Aston became a Football League referee alongside his career as a local headteacher. In 1946, he was the first league referee to wear – in place of the then-customary tweed jackets – a black uniform with white trim, which soon became the standard referee attire. The following year, after a match on a foggy London day, he introduced brightly coloured red and yellow linesmen's flags.

He officiated in the 1963 FA Cup final and later took overall charge of referees for the 1966, 1970 and 1974 World Cups. More famously, it was Aston who had the idea for red and yellow cards following the England versus Argentina match at the 1966 World

EAST

Cup. Jack Charlton had been booked by the German referee (verbally and in German) in the match but had not realised until he read about it later in the press. The story goes that Aston was driving home and stopped at a red light in Kensington. Inspired by the traffic lights, he came up with the idea of colour-coded cards to overcome language barriers and provide clarity to players and spectators alike as to when a player was being cautioned or sent off.

To be 'shown the red card' has become part of our common lexicon, and east London's Ken Aston was the originator.

Ken Aston had the idea for red and yellow cards while waiting at traffic lights

Harry Kane MBE

1993 –

Peter May Sports Centre,
135 Wadham Road, Walthamstow

E17 4HR

We arrive in Walthamstow, where we find a somewhat controversial statue of Harry Kane. Born locally and brought up within a 15-minute drive of Tottenham Hotspur's ground, Kane was destined to lead the club's frontline for over 12 years and become its all-time highest goal-scorer. He also tops England's goal-scoring list.

The statue, supported by Waltham Forest Council, is relatively basic with little accurate detail. After many years in storage, it has finally been installed in front of a mural at the rear of the Peter May Sports Centre in Walthamstow, where Harry Kane played as a boy with Ridgeway Rovers FC. The statue shows Kane, the 2018 FIFA World Cup Golden Boot winner, sitting on a bench in his England kit.

EAST

15

Beryl Swain

1936 – 2007

Wood Street, Walthamstow

E17 3GN

18 Grosvenor Park Road, Walthamstow

E17 9PG

Beryl Swain is pictured in 1962 before competing in the Isle of Man TT

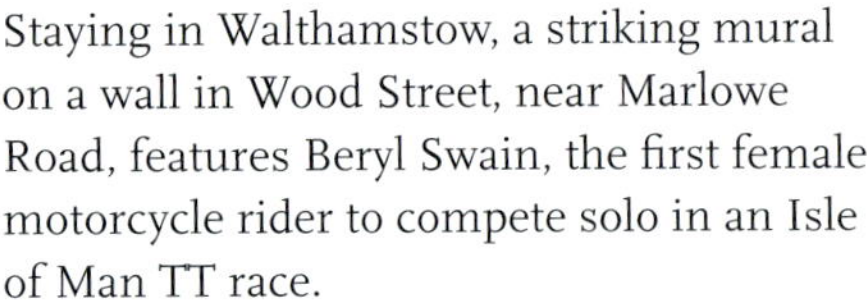

Staying in Walthamstow, a striking mural on a wall in Wood Street, near Marlowe Road, features Beryl Swain, the first female motorcycle rider to compete solo in an Isle of Man TT race.

Born nearby, Beryl met and married Eddie Swain, the owner of a motorcycle repair business, and they moved to a flat in Grosvenor Park Road. It is here that she is now celebrated by a plaque installed as part of the Waltham Forest Heritage scheme.

Swain began racing the new 50cc ultra-light motorbikes with great success, winning many trophies. It was, however, a male-dominated sport. She entered the Isle of Man TT race in the new class in 1962. The International Motorcycling Federation (IMF), wary of allowing female racers, imposed a minimum weight of 9st 6lbs on safety grounds (although only for this event). Swain intentionally put on weight and made the minimum requirement with the additional help of a lead-weighted belt. She was amongst the finishers in the race, but her international career came abruptly to an end. The IMF revoked Swain's licence and made the event male-only on the grounds that they were not prepared to risk injury or death to a female rider. It was never reinstated. For Swain this was "a matter of female prejudice under a thin veneer of safety first". It would be another 16 years before another female solo rider could compete.

In Walthamstow, Swain's pioneering story is celebrated – both by plaque and through this colourful mural by local artist Helen Bur depicting Swain at the peak of her racing prowess.

EAST

Beryl Swain was the first female motorcycle solo rider to compete in a TT race

16

Leyton Orient Football Club

Oliver Road, Leyton

E10 5NF

Coronation Gardens, Buckingham Road, Leyton

E10 5NL

Returning south from Walthamstow, we discover the story of Leyton Orient Football Club – a club not currently in the higher echelons of the sport but rich in sporting heritage.

In Oliver Road, by the ticket office for the current ground, a plaque records the club's formation as the Glyn Cricket Club by students of the local teacher training college. The football section was created in 1888 so that the cricket team could keep fit in the winter. They called themselves the Orient Football Club, apparently because one of the committee members worked for the Orient Steamship & Navigation Company. The 'Os' were born.

The name was changed to Clapton Orient FC when the club moved its ground. A further move was made to a greyhound-racing stadium in Millfields Road. Intriguingly, it was here that, in honour of Orient's patriotic lead in the Great War (*see far right*), the first visit by a member of the Royal Family to a Football League match (as opposed to an FA Cup final) was made when, in April 1921, the Prince of Wales (later King Edward VIII) watched the Os beat Notts County. The club would further change name to Leyton Orient

Three Os players would die at the Battle of the Somme and the War Memorial records their sacrifice

A First World War recruitment poster calls for volunteers to join the Footballers' Battalion

EAST

Leyton's War Memorial recalls the sacrifice of players of Clapton Orient FC

following the Second World War, having also relocated to Brisbane Road in 1937.

In Coronation Gardens, near the Brisbane Road ground, is the Leyton War Memorial. At the start of the First World War, the government's recruitment drive was aided by the formation of a volunteer battalion of footballers, officials and supporters – the 17th Battalion of the Middlesex Regiment (commonly known as the Footballers' Battalion). One of the first to sign up to serve in it was the captain of Clapton Orient FC, promptly followed by nine other members of the team.

Three of the club's players would die in the Battle of the Somme, and this War Memorial records their sacrifice and that of many others in the Leyton community.

17

Laurie Cunningham

1956 – 1989

Coronation Gardens,
Buckingham Road, Leyton

E10 5NG

We stay in Coronation Gardens, a stone's throw from Leyton Orient's Brisbane Road ground, where a fine bronze statue pays tribute to Laurie Cunningham – the first black footballer to play in a competitive senior international for England.

Born in Archway, Cunningham began his career at Leyton Orient and is regarded as the greatest player to have played for the club. A thrilling winger, his pace and flair made him a fan favourite during his three years with the Os before moving to West Bromwich Albion and later Real Madrid (becoming the first British player to transfer to the famous Spanish club). He was tragically killed in a car accident in Spain in 1989.

Cunningham is remembered also by plaques in nearby Kitchen Court off Brisbane Road and at his childhood home in Haringey (*see North London*). The statue here, by sculptor Graham Ibbeson, was unveiled in 2017. It was supported by Leyton Orient and 'Kick It Out', football's campaign body tasked with tackling racism. The plinth recalls Cunningham's words when dealing with abuse: "If I can get through this, maybe it will lead to others getting a fair chance."

EAST

Laurie Cunningham was a trailblazer for racial equality in football

18

Pickwick Bicycle Club

75 Downs Road, Hackney

E5 8DS

Heading towards central London, we come across a fascinating reminder of the start of a new craze in 19th century England – cycling.

It was in June 1870 at the Downs Hotel in Hackney that six enthusiasts with their new bicycles met and formed a cycling club amidst the excitement for the novel and evolving mode of transport. Still in existence today, it claims to be the oldest surviving cycling club in the world.

That initial meeting took place just two weeks after the death of Charles Dickens and the members named their new club after the author's famous work, *The Pickwick Papers*. Indeed, the club has continued as a lunch club celebrating England's great writer alongside its bicycle-related activities.

A commemorative plaque was first erected at the former hotel building in 1996 by the London Borough of Hackney. The building was converted into flats years later and the plaque lost. When the story was re-discovered, a replacement plaque was duly erected in 2014. Gratifyingly, members of the Pickwick Bicycle Club still enjoy their lunch celebrations to this day.

Pickwick Bicycle Club is the world's oldest surviving cycling club

Members of the Pickwick Bicycle Club pose for a photograph in 1886 with a variety of penny farthings and period bicycles

EAST

19

Walter Tull

1888 – 1918

Old Spotted Dog Ground,
212 Upton Lane, Forest Gate

E7 9NP

A plaque, with the Old Spotted Dog Ground in the background, proudly recalls Walter Tull and his first club

The story of Walter Tull, one of the first prominent black footballers in the English game, has been told earlier (*see North London*). Here, at the Old Spotted Dog Ground in Forest Gate, a new plaque was unveiled in 2025 at the ground where Tull started playing as an amateur in 1908 in the red and white stripes of Clapton FC. At that time the local *Football Star* newspaper called him "the catch of the season".

An inside forward of Afro-Caribbean descent, Tull was a leading player in a successful team that won the FA Amateur Cup before signing for Tottenham Hotspur the following season. In the First World War, he became one of the first black combat officers in the British Army. He was sadly killed in action.

The plaque itself has a story. In 2015, local Forest Gate residents erected an unofficial blue plaque on the gate at the ground without formal approval. Removed by the club, it was presumed lost – but later found several years later behind the bar in the ground's clubhouse, now occupied by Clapton Community FC. In 2025, a new information plaque was unveiled at the gate and the alleyway beside the ground was widened and re-named 'Walter Tull Way'.

Walter Tull began his career here at the Old Spotted Dog Ground

20

West Ham Utd's European champions

London Stadium, Queen Elizabeth Olympic Park, Stratford

E20 2ST

Continuing the story of West Ham United, we arrive at the club's new home – the London Stadium in Stratford. A link with past glories following the club's move from Upton Park is provided with a striking statue, by sculptor Ian Lander, which celebrates the club's memorable European Cup Winners' Cup victory in 1965.

Featured in larger-than-life size are **Bobby Moore OBE**, holding the trophy aloft; **Martin Peters MBE**, who made more than 300 appearances for West Ham and was once described by Alf Ramsey as the "complete midfielder" and "10 years ahead of his time"; and **Sir Geoff Hurst**, hat-trick scorer in England's World Cup victory and knight of the realm. All were homegrown, local players who progressed through the club's famous academy.

The names of the full team for the 1965 victory, as well as manager Ron Greenwood, appear on the sculpture's plinth. The club's fans understandably dream of achieving such success again.

The European Cup Winners' Cup win elevated West Ham to international prominence

21

Olympic Games 2012

Queen Elizabeth Olympic Park, Stratford

E20 2ST

Behold this new Olympic torch, the flames
that first blazed forth at Greece's early dawn:
Now give a rousing welcome to these Games,
on London's riverbanks reborn.

Above: The Olympic Rings from 2012 remain on display in the Queen Elizabeth Olympic Park

Below: London Mayor Boris Johnson recites the Pindaric ode (engraved in bronze, left) at an opening gala for London 2012

London's third staging of the Olympic Games took place in 2012, with the new Queen Elizabeth Olympic Park providing the central location. The memory of those exciting summer days – not least 'Super Saturday' when Team GB won three thrilling gold medals within 44 evening minutes inside the Olympic Stadium – live on. Around the park today, though, there are relatively few commemorative reminders.

Retained from 2012 and located now to the north of the park near the Velodrome are the five interlinked Olympic Rings, representing the union of the world's five continents and the gathering of athletes from around the world. Other similar Olympic Rings around London at the time of the Games have been recycled for new uses. Here, however, they remain a distinctive and colourful feature.

Embedded in a path near a bridge close to the Olympic Stadium (now West Ham's London Stadium), an unusual circular bronze plaque is engraved with an ode, known as a Pindaric ode, composed for the 2012 Olympics by Oxford academic Armand D'Angour. The ode was gleefully recited in both English and Greek by then-Mayor Boris Johnson at an IOC gala celebrating the handover of the Olympic Games to London. In English, its opening lines proclaim: "Behold this new Olympic torch, the flames that first blazed forth at Greece's early dawn: Now give a rousing welcome to the Games, on London's riverbanks reborn."

EAST

Above: Jessica Ennis, Greg Rutherford and Mo Farah all won gold medals during the dramatic evening of 'Super Saturday'

The Olympic Bell, which was rung at the opening ceremony, is now hung outside the London Stadium

At the opening of the 2012 Games, the Olympic Bell was loudly rung. The largest tuned bell in the world, it is inscribed with a line from Shakespeare's *The Tempest*: "Be not afeard, the isle is full of noises." The bell will, though, apparently not be heard again – to avoid disturbing those now living around the park.

Memories and commemorative reminders of London's 2012 Olympic Games are vivid and distinctive – and some are unusual

ROYA
TUESDA
TERR
DAVE ST
LONDO

SOUTH-EAST LONDON

Henry Cooper was the most popular British boxer of the 20th century. Having been born, grown up and trained in the area, he is now celebrated by plaque and statue among his people in South-East London.

SOUTH-EAST LONDON

South-East London is associated immediately with The Oval, a truly iconic venue in sport. Cricket's heritage is celebrated by distinctive reminders not only here but also in the surrounding areas, where many of the game's great names made their homes.

Also in South-East London we recall famous names and vivid moments in athletics, from the historic sub-four-minute mile to Britain's greatest decathlete, as well as echoes of *Chariots of Fire*. Southwark was the childhood home of two great England footballers, and in West Norwood we pay tribute to the creator of the FA Cup and one of the most influential figures in the development of British sport. We also remember, in Eltham, the founder of one of the world's oldest annual contested sporting events and, in Blackheath, the early days of rugby union and its separation from association football.

Here in South-East London we also salute no fewer than four Sirs, four sporting knights of the realm, as we enjoy this feast of sporting history.

1. **Daley Thompson**
2. **First Test match on English soil**
3. **The Ashes**
4. **Sir Jack Hobbs**
5. **More legends of The Oval:**
   Bobby Abel, Tom Richardson,
   Sir Len Hutton, Sir Don Bradman
6. **The first FA Cup final**
7. **Bobby Abel**
8. **Sir Henry Cooper**
9. **Kenny Sansom**
10. **Rio Ferdinand**
11. **Lord David Sheppard**
12. **Edgar Kail**
13. **Sir Henry Cotton**
14. **Sam Mussabini**
15. **Wilfried Zaha**
16. **Charles Alcock**
17. **Joanna Rowsell**
18. **David Weir**
19. **Gordon Pirie**
20. **Sir Roger Bannister**
21. **CB Fry**
22. **WG Grace**
23. **Sir Henry Cooper**
24. **Eric Liddell**
25. **Thomas Doggett**
26. **Blackheath Football Club**
27. **Sam Bartram**
28. **Tom Cribb**

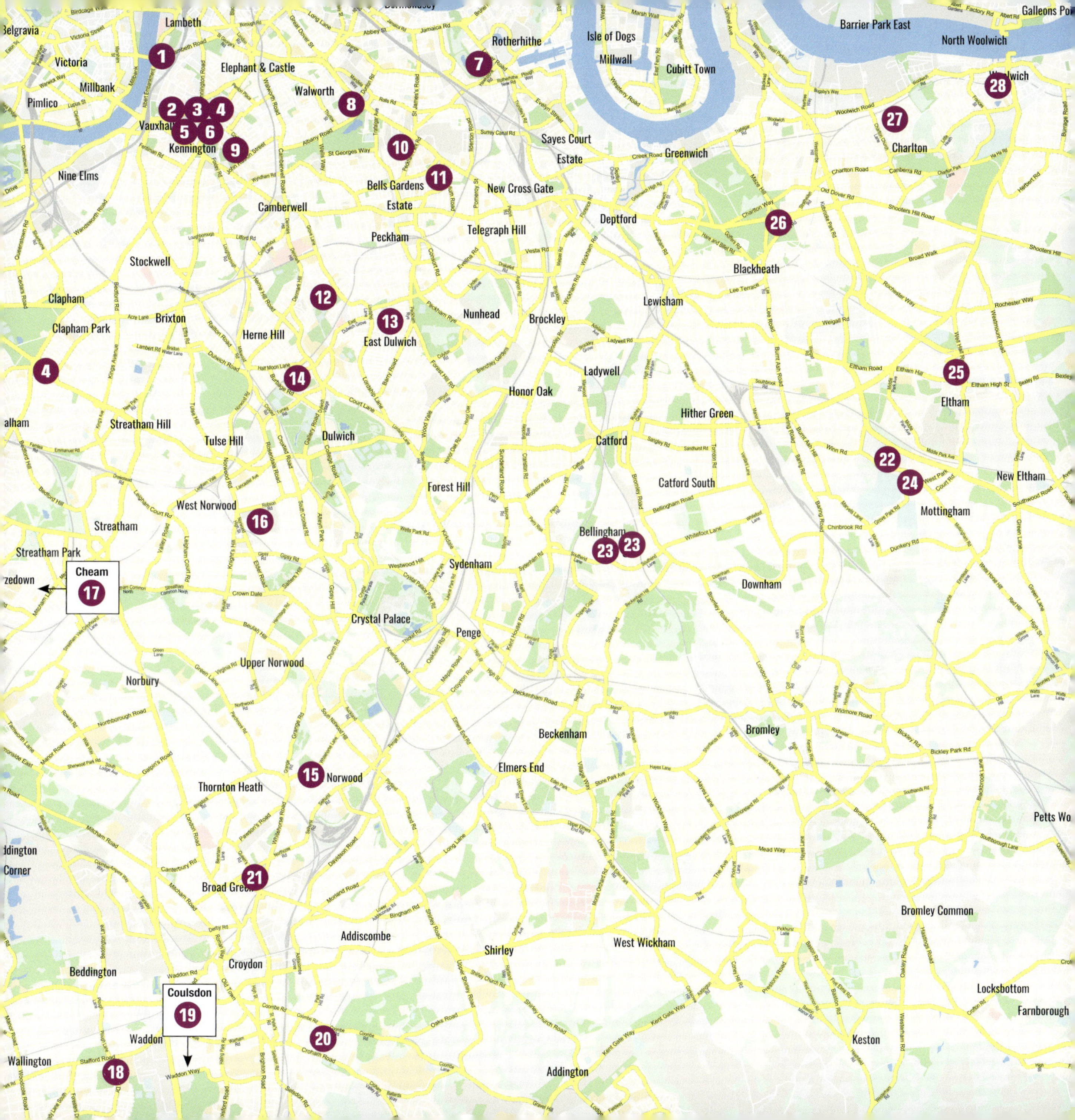

Belgravia
Lambeth
Victoria
Millbank
Pimlico
Vauxhall
Kennington
Elephant & Castle
Walworth
Rotherhithe
Isle of Dogs
Millwall
Cubitt Town
Barrier Park East
North Woolwich
Galleons Po
Woolwich
Nine Elms
Camberwell
Bells Gardens Estate
New Cross Gate
Sayes Court Estate
Greenwich
Charlton
Deptford
Blackheath
Peckham
Telegraph Hill
Stockwell
Clapham
Clapham Park
Brixton
Herne Hill
East Dulwich
Nunhead
Brockley
Lewisham
Ladywell
Honor Oak
Hither Green
Eltham
Streatham Hill
Tulse Hill
Dulwich
Catford
Catford South
New Eltham
Mottingham
Forest Hill
West Norwood
Streatham
Streatham Park
Bellingham
Sydenham
Downham
Cheam
Crystal Palace
Penge
Upper Norwood
Norbury
Beckenham
Bromley
Elmers End
Thornton Heath
Norwood
Petts Wo
Broad Green
Bromley Common
Addiscombe
Shirley
West Wickham
Croydon
Beddington
Coulsdon
Locksbottom
Farnborough
Waddon
Keston
Wallington
Addington
1
2
3
4
5
6
7
8
9
10
11
12
13
14
15
16
17
18
19
20
21
22
23
24
25
26
27
28

1

Daley Thompson CBE

1958 –

Southbank Centre, Belvedere Road, Southwark

SE1 8XX

We start on a pavement on the south-west side of the South Bank's Queen Elizabeth Hall. A group of tiled (and tired) mosaics feature portraits from sport and entertainment with no obvious connections. The most distinctive and recognisable sporting figure is Daley Thompson.

Born in Notting Hill, the son of a British-Nigerian father and Scottish mother, he became Britain's greatest decathlete – winning gold medals at both the 1980 and 1984 Olympic Games and breaking the world record on four occasions.

Sport was, from an early age, the outlet for Thompson's energy and ambition. Football attracted, but his speed, strength and endurance made him a superb all-round athlete. Clearly a rising star, aged 19 he won the decathlon at the 1978 Commonwealth Games. He then became the dominant decathlete of his generation and only the second to claim the gold medal at two Olympic Games. His colourful personality added to his appeal.

Fading and not particularly artful, this mosaic is nevertheless a reminder of one of Britain's finest Olympians.

Below: Daley Thompson, twice Olympic decathlon gold medallist, competes in Seoul in 1988

Thompson's speed, strength and endurance made him a superb all-round athlete

SOUTH-EAST

2

The first Test match on English soil

1888

The Kia Oval, Kennington

SE11 5SS

SURREY COUNTY CRICKET CLUB
THIS PLAQUE
HONOURS THE MATCH
PLAYED BETWEEN
ENGLAND AND AUSTRALIA
AT THE OVAL, FROM THE
6th-8th SEPTEMBER 1880
THE FIRST TEST MATCH
ON ENGLISH SOIL
England won by five wickets
WG Grace scored 152, becoming
England's first centurion
D.R. London S.E.5

We move to the The Oval (now formally the Kia Oval) where, amongst many reminders of cricket's rich history, a plaque by the main Hobbs Gates recalls the game now deemed "the first Test match on English soil".

A tour to Australia arranged by James Lillywhite had led to the match in Melbourne in 1877 which, retrospectively, is recognised as the first 'Test' match – won by Australia. A similar tour the following year was, however, marred by an ugly protest against the English in Sydney following a run-out umpiring decision.

With a background of some continued bad feeling, in 1880 a match between England and a visiting Australian team was hastily arranged at The Oval by Lord Harris. More than 20,000 spectators attended the first day. They witnessed a debut century by WG Grace, who hit 152 runs (thereby becoming England's first Test centurion) to give the hosts a commanding lead. England slumped in the second innings but held on to register a five-wicket victory.

Significantly, the animosity had been overcome and this match did much to cement the custom of cricket tours between England and Australia, a tradition that remains a highlight of the sporting calendar.

The match at The Oval did much to cement cricket tours between England and Australia

An illustration of the England vs Australia Test match at The Oval in 1880

3

The Ashes

1882

The Kia Oval, Kennington

SE11 5SS

Another plaque near the Hobbs Gates recalls the famous loss that an England XI suffered at The Oval against the touring Australian team in 1882. The match, completed on 29 August, was the first time England had lost on home soil. Needing only 85 runs to win, England collapsed in their second innings and fell short by eight runs. The following day, *The Sporting Times* printed a satirical obituary for the death of English cricket: "Deeply lamented by a large circle of sorrowing friends and acquaintances. R.I.P. – N.B. The body will be cremated and the ashes taken to Australia."

Before the subsequent tour to Australia, England's captain Ivo Bligh vowed "to regain those ashes". After England had indeed won the series, a small urn was presented to Bligh at a social event in Melbourne. Legend (sadly unproven) has it that the urn contained the ashes of a wooden bail. A personal gift to Bligh, the urn was passed to the MCC by his widow after his death. The original now has pride of place in the MCC Museum at Lord's, and a replica is presented to the winning team at the conclusion of each Test series between the two nations.

The term 'the Ashes' did not actually gain wide acceptance until the early 1900s but the iconic symbol of cricket's oldest and keenest international rivalry originated from a match here at The Oval.

Left: An 1883 portrait of England's captain, Ivo Bligh, who famously vowed to "regain those ashes"

Right: The original Ashes urn is on display in the MCC Museum

"The body will be cremated and the ashes taken to Australia"

4

Sir Jack Hobbs

1882 – 1963

The Kia Oval, Kennington

SE11 5SS

17 Englewood Road, Clapham

SW12 9PA

The main entrance to The Oval celebrates one of cricket's all-time greats. John 'Jack' Berry Hobbs was England's finest batsman in the first decades both before and after the First World War. Nicknamed 'the Master', Hobbs retired in 1934 and Surrey honoured its legendary batsman by naming the gates in front of the main pavilion 'the Hobbs Gates', elegantly designed "in honour of a great Surrey & England cricketer".

Hobbs provided the batting backbone of Surrey and England for well over two decades. He scored more runs (61,760) and more centuries (199) in first-class cricket than any other player in the history of the game – nearly all from the top of the batting order. Hobbs's career was interrupted by the First World War. Although his most spectacular batting period probably came before the start of hostilities, the majority of his centuries were scored after he had turned 40 years old. He remains the oldest man to score a Test century, having scored 142, aged 46, against Australia in 1929. In 1953, he also became the first cricketer – and the first 'professional' sportsman – to be knighted.

In 1986, a plaque was placed at his former home in Englewood Road in Clapham, where Hobbs lived between 1912 and 1927, the years of his greatest fame. His name sits proudly in the pantheon of cricket's all-time greats.

The great Jack Hobbs in action at the crease in 1935

SOUTH-EAST

The main entrance at The Oval celebrates one of cricket's all-time greats

5

More legends of The Oval

The Kia Oval, Kennington

SE11 5SS

The richness of its cricket history is evident all around The Oval, its grounds and museum (*see London's sporting museums & tours*).

The various entrances to the ground (in addition to the Hobbs Gates) have been named in honour of various Surrey captains: Stuart Surridge, John Edrich MBE, Alec Stewart OBE, Adam Hollioake and Nat Sciver-Brunt. Inside, walls and columns display photo montages of past Surrey icons – from Jim Laker and Ken Barrington to Mark Butcher and Kevin Pietersen, as well as many more. The main pavilion itself has been renamed in honour of Micky Stewart OBE, the esteemed former Surrey captain and England coach and manager. We focus here on four other legendary players recalled around the ground.

Two distinctive player plaques on the pavilion wall catch the historian's eye. One records the achievements of **Bobby Abel** (1857–1936). Abel was 'the Guv'nor' at The Oval, a prolific run-scorer and one of the most well-known and popular cricketers of his age. Born in Rotherhithe, his cricket beginnings are also proudly celebrated in Southwark Park (*see page 179*).

Another plaque recalls **Tom Richardson** (1870–1912). Richardson, born in Byfleet, was a legendary fast bowler for Surrey and England. His glory years were the mid-1890s, when he took an extraordinary 1,005 wickets during a four-year spell from 1894, including 290 in one glorious summer. In 1963, Neville Cardus selected him as one of his 'Six Giants of the Wisden Century'.

Below: Batsman Bobby Abel (left) and fast bowler Tom Richardson (right) are both legends of the game

SOUTH-EAST

Members and their guests enjoy the fine view from the Micky Stewart Members' Pavilion

Hutton's 364 remains the highest Test innings by an Englishman

Len Hutton's record-breaking innings is cleverly recalled in brick near the pavilion

More legends of The Oval

SE11 5SS

continued

The Oval has been the scene of many historic cricket moments and occasions. Two of the most memorable are recalled here, still with emotion and admiration.

Yorkshire opener **Sir Len Hutton** (1916–1990) was at the heart of England's team in the mid-20th century. In 1938, he scored 364 runs here against Australia in a famous innings which spanned more than 13 hours of play. It was then the highest individual score in Test history, and it remains the highest Test innings by an Englishman. In 1952, Hutton was appointed England's first-ever 'professional' captain. Under his leadership, England did not lose a Test series. He was knighted in 1956. Near the pavilion at The Oval, a large striking red brick bas-relief (*above*) by sculptor Walter Ritchie depicts the great batsman in flowing action and recalls that record-breaking Test innings in 1938.

Inside the main pavilion, The Bradman Doors commemorate the final Test innings of **Sir Don Bradman** (1908–2001), generally acknowledged as the world's all-time greatest batsman. At The Oval in August 1948, and amidst scenes of overwhelming emotion, the Australian misread leg-spinner Eric Hollies's googly and was bowled without scoring, leaving him with a tantalising – but still extraordinary – Test batting average of 99.94.

A stunned silence around the ground gave way to tumultuous applause as Bradman, bat under his arm, made his way to the pavilion and walked through the doors that today bear his name.

The Oval gave way to tumultuous applause as Bradman, bat under his arm, made his way to the pavilion

Don Bradman is bowled out for a duck in his final Test innings at The Oval

6

The first FA Cup final

The Kia Oval, Kennington

SE11 5SS

The historic cricket venue of The Oval has also played an important role in the history of other sports – including as the site of the first final of football's FA Cup.

The competition was created in 1871, largely thanks to Charles Alcock (*see page 188*). The uniquitous Alcock was also secretary of the Surrey County Cricket Club, and The Oval was chosen as the venue for the competition's first final. Alcock also happened to be the captain of The Wanderers, who beat The Royal Engineers 1-0 in the final thanks to a goal scored by Morton Betts.

Intriguingly, Betts played under the pseudonym 'AH Chequer' (for 'A Harrow Chequer'); educated at Harrow, he also played for The Harrow Chequers. The latter had entered but did not play their first-round match. Betts was therefore not considered 'cup-tied' and was able to play in the final and enter the history books.

The Oval would continue to be the venue for international football and FA Cup finals for several years, hosting its last final in 1892. Fittingly, a plaque on the main pavilion wall recalls that historic first final.

A newspaper illustration depicts an early football match at The Oval, with England taking on Scotland in 1878

The Oval would continue to be the venue for international football and FA Cup finals

SOUTH-EAST

7

Bobby Abel

1857 – 1936

Pavilion Café, Southwark Park,
Hawkstone Road, Southwark

SE16 2UA

At Southwark Park we recall again Surrey's Bobby Abel. Born in Rotherhithe, Abel was probably the best-known cricketer after WG Grace for the two decades at the end of the 19th century and the start of the 20th.

An opening batsman, small in height and unorthodox in his attacking style, he was one of the most prolific run-scorers of his time. His 357 not out in 1899 at The Oval (where a pavilion plaque also honours the great batsman) was the ground's highest first-class score until Len Hutton's record-breaking innings 39 years later. He was also the first England batsman to 'carry his bat' throughout an entire innings. "He gathers runs like blackberries everywhere he goes," declared his fellow England international, CB Fry.

Abel's skills were first spotted while playing club cricket here in Southwark Park. A plaque placed by Southwark Council, at the former site of the park's cricket pavilion, is a reminder of one of cricket's great early stars.

"He gathers runs like blackberries everywhere he goes"

Bobby Abel – who was nicknamed 'the Guv'nor' – poses for a sporting portrait in 1894

SOUTH-EAST

8

Sir Henry Cooper

1934 – 2011

322 Old Kent Road, Southwark

SE1 5UE

Britain has produced many fine boxing heavyweights, but none have been more popular than Henry Cooper. British, Commonwealth and European heavyweight champion, he is affectionately recalled here in the Old Kent Road, as well as elsewhere in South-East London (*see page 196*) and indeed also near Wembley (*see West London*).

A vivid sporting memory of the 1960s is that night, in June 1963, when 'Enry's 'Ammer – Cooper's trademark left hook – sent a stunned Cassius Clay onto his back in the fourth round at a packed Wembley Stadium. Sloped against the ropes, Clay was 'saved by the bell'. In the next round, Cooper's eye was badly cut and the referee stopped the fight to award Clay victory. Cooper's chance was gone but his courage and engaging honesty won the admiration and affection of countless millions.

Here, above the former Thomas à Becket pub on the Old Kent Road (now a Vietnamese food outlet), was the gym where Cooper trained in the 1960s and 1970s and developed his famous punch. A blue plaque for the site was voted for by the people of Southwark and unveiled by Sir Henry himself in 2008.

Henry Cooper in training at the Thomas à Becket gym in 1969

It was here that Cooper developed his famous 'Enry's 'Ammer punch

9

Kenny Sansom

1958 –

Morton House, Royal Road, Southwark

SE17 3NW

Southwark Council, supported by the Southwark Heritage Association, proudly celebrates many nationally recognised heroes associated with the borough. On a council block on the corner of Royal Road and Otto Street, a blue plaque voted for by local people honours Kenny Sansom.

Brought up on the Brandon Estate by his mother, he shone in the youth team at Crystal Palace before joining Arsenal in 1980. Stylish, strong and consistent, Sansom was at the heart of the team's famous defence and, with 86 caps, is regarded as one of England's best-ever full-backs.

10

Rio Ferdinand MBE

1978 –

Millbrook House, Friary Estate, Peckham Park Road, Peckham

SE15 6TG

In Peckham there is another plaque erected by Southwark Council in honour of a local footballer following a vote by the local community. This one honours Rio Ferdinand, one of England's finest-ever central defenders.

Ferdinand was brought up here on the Friary Estate in Peckham, and his father took him to football training nearby. It was there that his talent was spotted by West Ham and he swiftly joined their youth team. Making his first-team debut in 1996, he became a fan favourite at West Ham before moving first to Leeds United and then to Manchester United, winning 14 trophies during a 12-year stint at Old Trafford.

The plaque, on the side of an estate building, overlooks a patch of grass and a concrete playground where Ferdinand played as a boy.

11

Lord David Sheppard

1929 – 2005

12 Asylum Road, Peckham

SE15 2RL

Back to cricket, a plaque here in Peckham at the former home of David Sheppard recalls the only ordained minister to have played Test cricket.

Sheppard started to play first-class cricket at Cambridge University with great accomplishment, making his Test debut in 1950 while still at university. In 1952 he topped the English batting averages before later captaining Sussex. In 1954, he captained England in two Tests against Pakistan, in the absence of Len Hutton.

While focusing on his ministry career, Sheppard's Test career dimmed. He was, however, recalled in 1956 to play Australia in the fourth Test at Old Trafford and scored a fine century. Taking a sabbatical from his church mission, Sheppard toured Australia in 1962/63 under captain Ted Dexter. Following his unfortunate dropping of a couple of catches in the field against England's arch rivals, Fred Trueman memorably declared: "Pretend it's Sunday Reverend, and keep your hands together."

Sheppard became Bishop of Woolwich in 1969 and subsequently Bishop of Liverpool in 1975 (becoming the youngest diocesan bishop in England). A lifelong advocate for social reform, he was elevated in 1998 to a life peerage in the House of Lords. Here, in south-east London, a plaque placed by the Peckham Society recalls the home where this outstanding individual lived for six years.

"Pretend it's Sunday Reverend, and keep your hands together"

SOUTH-EAST

Left: Reverend David Sheppard plays cricket with young members of his flock in 1957

Above: Sheppard strides onto the pitch as Sussex captain at Hove in 1954

12

Edgar Kail

1900 – 1976

Champion Hill Stadium,
Edgar Kail Way, East Dulwich

SE22 8BD

We move to East Dulwich and a plaque commemorating a local football hero who was the last player outside the principal leagues or divisions to play for the full England team.

Born in Camberwell, Edgar Kail signed for Dulwich Hamlet FC of the Isthmian League in 1915 as a 15-year-old. An inside forward, he played until 1933 with the club, twice winning the FA Amateur Cup. Kail won three caps for England in 1929. A committed amateur, he declined many offers from professional clubs.

In 2003, this plaque was unveiled by Southwark Council on the wall of the club's stadium as part of its 'Voted by the People' initiative. It states that Kail was the "last amateur footballer to play for England". Purists may argue that this was actually Bernard Joy of Arsenal in 1936. However, it is highly unlikely that any other non-league player, or indeed amateur, will ever succeed Kail in playing for the full national team.

A bas-relief plaque on the same stadium wall celebrates the founder of Dulwich Hamlet FC, **Lorraine 'Pa' Wilson** (1865–1924). A lifelong figure within the club, the story goes that the last words he heard before he died informed him that his Dulwich 'boys' had won that day with a hat-trick scored by his favourite 'son' – Edgar Kail.

Above and below: Plaques at Champion Hill Stadium recall legendary figures in the history of Dulwich Hamlet FC

Edgar Kail, forever amateur, declined offers from many professional clubs

13

Sir Henry Cotton

1907 – 1987

47 Crystal Palace Road, East Dulwich

SE22 9EX

Still in Dulwich, we celebrate Henry Cotton – Britain's finest golfer of the first half of the 20th century. The first golfer to be knighted, he is remembered by a blue plaque erected by English Heritage at his former family home.

Brought up here in Crystal Palace Road, he practised his swing in the back garden where his father, a keen golfer, had set up training nets. Aged 27, Cotton won the Open Championship at Sandwich in 1934, ending a decade of American victories. A second Open victory followed in 1937.

With his career having been interrupted by the Second World War, he gained his third Open victory in 1948. How much more might he have achieved if war had not intervened? After his retirement from competition, Cotton became a successful golf course architect. He also notably established the Golf Foundation, helping youngsters to get started in the sport. He was knighted in 1988.

A compelling personality, his fame significantly elevated the status of the professional golfer in Great Britain.

Cotton practised his swing in the back garden here

Henry Cotton swinging freely in 1932, two years before the first of his three Open victories

14

Sam Mussabini

1867 – 1927

84 Burbage Road, Herne Hill

SE24 9HE

Echoes of *Chariots of Fire* can be heard here in Herne Hill.

Blackheath-born and of Syrian, Turkish, Italian and French heritage, Scipio Africanus Mussabini was generally called 'Sam' after his initials. Skilled at many sports, he became a well-known athletics coach. Appointed as the first professional coach to London's Polytechnic Harriers, he trained many leading athletes of the day.

Famously, with his distinctive methods focusing on running style and length of stride, he coached Harold Abrahams to his gold medal triumph in the 100 metres at the 1924 Olympic Games in Paris. It is a story dramatised in the well-known film. His words of advice to Abrahams before the Olympic final were said to be: "Only think of two things – the report of the pistol, and the tape. When you hear the one, just run like hell until you reach the other."

Mussabini is recalled by an English Heritage plaque erected in 2012 at his former home in Burbage Road. It lies, appropriately, within sight of the cycling and athletics stadium at Herne Hill where he coached Abrahams to Olympic glory.

Sam Mussabini (right) coaches Harold Abrahams prior to the 1924 Olympics

Echoes of *Chariots of Fire* can be heard here in Herne Hill

SOUTH-EAST

Wilfried Zaha

1992 –

Park Road, Selhurst

SE25 6PU

Among the capital's growing number of football street murals, one of the most striking is located near Crystal Palace's stadium at Selhurst Park.

Designed by the MurWalls collective and supported by the club, it celebrates Eagles legend Wilfried Zaha and his achievements in over 300 appearances as a winger in the red and blue of Palace. The mural is not far from Rothesay Road, where the winger was raised. One image features his iconic celebration after a goal in the Championship play-off semi-finals and the memorable commentary line: "Zaha… Oh Yes!"

A vibrant mural of Wilfried Zaha is painted on the wall of a house near Crystal Palace's Selhurst Park stadium

16

Charles Alcock

1842 – 1907

West Norwood Cemetery,
Norwood Road, West Norwood

SE27 9JU

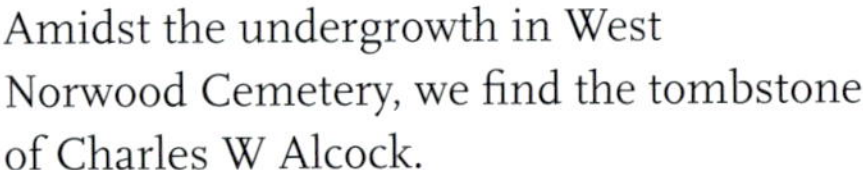

Amidst the undergrowth in West Norwood Cemetery, we find the tombstone of Charles W Alcock.

Association football was still in its infancy when Alcock became honorary secretary of the FA. An early initiative to promote international football came when, in 1870, he suggested that teams of Scottish and English players should compete against each other. His next major proposal came in 1871, namely that "a Challenge Cup" should be established "for which all clubs belonging to the Association should be invited to compete". The FA Cup became the world's first-ever national football competition and transformed the game in England.

Alcock also helped to shape the sport of cricket. From 1872 he was the secretary of Surrey CCC at The Oval, which became – in effect – the first national sports centre. It not only staged the first cricket Test match in England but also the first England vs Scotland rugby match south of the border, as well as several subsequent internationals and many early FA Cup finals.

In 1885, Alcock played a further significant role in football when he successfully argued that the FA should allow 'professionals' to play in competitions (at first, subject to residential qualifications). It was enough to prevent the kind of major split that had divided rugby.

Here, in West Norwood Cemetery, we pay respect to this major figure in the development of British sport. His grave was rededicated in 1999. Included on the tombstone, symbolically, is a carving of the FA Cup trophy.

Right: Charles Alcock's tombstone (left) incorporates an image of the original FA Cup trophy

SOUTH-EAST

Charles Alcock has been called 'the Father of Modern Sport'

17

Joanna Rowsell MBE

1988 –

Ewell Road, Cheam

SM3 8BU

A gold-painted post box can be found in Cheam in honour of Joanna Rowsell.

Rowsell was a member of the world record-breaking British cycling squad that won the women's team pursuit at the London 2012 Olympics – a gold-medal feat repeated in Rio in 2016. Her record also includes multiple World, European and Commonwealth championships.

Rowsell grew up in Cheam and attended the nearby Nonsuch High School for Girls. It was here that British Cycling talent scouts identified her potential. She later said she only took part to avoid a maths lesson!

18

David Weir CBE

1979 –

Mollison Drive, Wallington

SM6 9BY

Born in Wallington, near Sutton, David Weir (nicknamed 'the Weirwolf') is probably Britain's greatest male wheelchair athlete.

No fewer than four gold-painted post boxes can be found in the area in honour of his victories in four different Paralympic events at London 2012. One in Mollison Drive, near Spitfire Park, is in recognition of his win in the T54 men's marathon. His victories in the 800m, 1500m and 5000m are celebrated by post boxes elsewhere in Wallington.

Weir, born with a spinal cord transection that left him unable to use his legs, had previously won two gold medals at the 2008 Paralympic Games. He also won the wheelchair event at the London Marathon an astonishing eight times. Having retired in 2024, David Weir ranks as an all-time outstanding Paralympic athlete.

19

Gordon Pirie

1931 – 1991

194 Brighton Road, Coulsdon

CR5 2NF

Affixed to the frontage of the Coulsdon Club is a blue plaque, erected by the Bourne Society, celebrating Gordon Pirie.

Pirie was the country's outstanding middle and long-distance runner of the 1950s. He broke five world records at various distances and won a silver medal in the 5000 metres at the 1956 Olympic Games in Melbourne, finishing behind only his great rival, Vladimir Kuts from the Soviet Union. Pirie's dramatic races with Kuts and Czech Emil Zátopek, many shown on the black-and-white television of the day, are vivid sporting memories of the period.

Gordon Pirie grew up in Coulsdon and ran for South London Harriers. A relentless trainer and a strong and charismatic character, he is regarded as the forerunner of modern middle-distance running in this country. The plaque here at a popular members' club records local pride in this groundbreaking athlete.

Gordon Pirie, five-time world record breaker, on the running track in 1956

Pirie's dramatic races are vivid sporting memories of the 1950s

20

Sir Roger Bannister

1929 – 2018

Royal Russell School, Coombe Lane, Croydon

CR9 5BX

Moving to Croydon, we discover another tribute to the historic achievement of athlete Roger Bannister. On 6 May 1954, Bannister broke the four-minute barrier for the mile. It was a success that provided a major boost to the country's post-war morale.

Bannister's triumph is celebrated elsewhere (*see West London* for his former training ground and *Central London* for his recognition in Westminster Abbey). It also inspired the world-renowned Finnish sculptor, Eino. A keen runner himself, Eino created this striking sculpture in 2004 in his studio in America – not as a commission but purely inspired by his admiration for the great British athlete. Although Bannister himself did not have any connections with Royal Russell School in Croydon, the sculpture has – since May 2008 – been a source of inspiration for students and visitors in the grounds at the school where Eino had previously spent some time teaching.

Full of raw texture and expression, the life-size bronze sculpture – entitled 'Paradigm' – captures the moment when Bannister, face white and drawn, is about to breast the tape at the end of his legendary run. It represents a supreme moment when a barrier was broken and the sporting world changed.

This sculpture represents a supreme moment when a barrier was broken and the sporting world changed

Roger Bannister bursts through the tape at the end of his historic run, a moment captured in bronze (far left) by world-renowned sculptor, Eino

21

CB Fry

1872 – 1956

144 St James's Road, Croydon

CR0 2UY

If ever there was an all-round talented sportsman, it was Charles Burgess ('CB') Fry. Born here in Croydon and educated at Repton School and Oxford, his list of achievements is astonishing and unsurpassed.

Fry is probably best remembered for his career as a cricketer. He scored more than 30,000 first-class runs (at an average of 50) and captained England (with no Tests lost under his captaincy). "I had only one stroke maybe – but it went to 10 different parts of the ground," he once famously quipped. He also played football for Southampton (reaching the FA Cup final in 1902) and represented England, as well as equalling the world long jump record in 1892.

Fry was also a distinguished diplomat, teacher and writer. He was reputedly even offered the kingship of Albania. He spent more than 40 years as director of a youth training ship, for which he was made an honorary captain in the Royal Navy Reserve.

We have already visited a plaque at Fry's former home in Hendon (*see North London*). This one is located at his place of birth in St James's Road (then Edinburgh Villas) and was erected by English Heritage.

If ever there was an all-round talented sportsman, it was CB Fry

Extraordinary sporting all-rounder CB Fry demonstrates his cricketing prowess

SOUTH-EAST

22

WG Grace

1848 – 1915

Fairmount Residential Care Home, Mottingham Lane, Mottingham

SE9 3NG

Legendary batsman WG Grace in action in 1900

Diverting north to Mottingham, near Bromley, we pay further respects to WG Grace, whose monumental contribution to cricket over four decades we have already celebrated at Lord's (*see North London*).

Towards the end of his extraordinary career, Grace moved to Sydenham. A blue plaque was erected at his former home there in 1963, but the property was later demolished. Salvaged, it has since been placed on the front of the house in Mottingham (now a residential care home) where Grace and his wife, Agnes, moved in 1909 after his retirement from first-class cricket.

It was in the garden here in 1915, during the First World War, that he suffered a stroke from which he never recovered. It is said that distress caused by Zeppelin raids contributed to his stroke. Grace is reported to have complained that, unlike the deliveries from fast bowlers, the bombs being dropped were a threat that he could not see coming.

The 'Great Cricketer' saw fast deliveries coming more easily than Zeppelin bombs

SOUTH-EAST

23

Sir Henry Cooper

1934 – 2011

Randlesdown Road, Bellingham

SE6 2AH

120 Farmstead Road, Bellingham

SE6 3EA

Henry Cooper – Britain's most popular boxing champion of the 20th century – is celebrated across several sites in south-east London.

A plaque off the Old Kent Road (*see page 180*) recalls the gym where Cooper trained. Since 2022, a fine life-size statue by sculptor Carl Payne has stood on the corner where Randlesdown Road meets Bromley Road in Bellingham, close to the council estate where Cooper grew up and where a plaque has been erected outside his early home.

Cooper's professional career lasted 17 years. He fought 55 fights, winning 40 of them – the majority by knockout. He won the British and Commonwealth titles in 1959 and added the European title in 1968. Cooper retained his British title for over 12 years.

Known for his warmth and humour, Cooper's far-reaching popularity long endured. He was the first person to be twice voted BBC Sports Personality of the Year (in 1967 and 1970) and amongst the first sportsmen to be used for product endorsement – in the black-and-white TV age – most famously for Brut aftershave, advising men to "splash it all over!" In 2000 he became the first, and so far only, British boxer to receive a knighthood.

Here in Bellingham, Cooper is amongst his people, proudly displaying his record three Lonsdale belts – earned by winning and succesfully defending his British title.

Our 'Enry will be long remembered

Below left: Henry Cooper, age 23, in 1957

Below: The house in Bellingham where Cooper grew up

SOUTH-EAST

24

Eric Liddell

1902 – 1945

Eric Liddell Sports Centre,
Grove Park Road, Mottingham

SE9 4QF

Eric Liddell, with his distinctive running style, is pictured in 1924 – shortly after his Olympic triumph

Returning to Mottingham, we head to Eltham College and its Eric Liddell Sports Centre – named in memory of Scotland's hero and winner of Olympic gold in Paris in 1924. Inside, pupils and visitors (outside college hours) can view a statue sculpted by Lesley Pover. It powerfully captures Liddell's distinctive head-back, lung-bursting running style and evokes the sounds and images from the celebrated *Chariots of Fire* film.

Born in Tientsin in north-east China, where his Scottish parents were missionaries, Liddell went to boarding school here at Eltham College for more than a decade before going to Edinburgh University. Although a good rugby player, athletics was his real strength and he qualified to represent Britain in the 1924 Olympics at 100 metres and 200 metres. However, the heats for the 100 metres, his best event, were scheduled for a Sunday. Contrary to the plot of the famous film, Liddell knew this ahead of the Games and he refused to run on the Sabbath. Instead, he was entered for the 400 metres. Surprising the favourites who expected him to flag over the longer distance, the flying Scotsman gloriously won the gold medal in a world record time.

After the Olympics, Liddell returned to China to become a missionary. After the Japanese invaded Manchuria in 1943, he was interned in a concentration camp in Weifang. Two years later, aged 43, he died from a brain tumour at the camp just five months before it was liberated.

A 'Sportsman and Evangelist', Liddell's memory is still recalled at Eltham College and throughout Scotland.

"The secret of my success over 400 metres is that I run the first 200 metres as fast as I can. Then for the second 200 metres, with God's help, I run faster"

25

Thomas Doggett

c1640 – 1721

St John the Baptist Church,
Eltham High Street, Eltham

SE9 1DH

We stay nearby in Eltham and return to the early days of watermen on the River Thames. Here, Thomas Doggett is recalled with a plaque on the front wall of St. John's Church, where he was buried.

Born in Dublin, Doggett was a well-known Irish-born comic actor and joint manager of Drury Lane Theatre. In 1715, with the River Thames bustling with activity, he initiated the Coat and Badge Race for young watermen who had not exceeded their apprenticeship by more than 12 months. He established the race (for individual scullers) in honour of the House of Hanover and the anniversary of the accession to the throne of King George I in 1714. In his will, Doggett left instructions and provision to ensure that the race would continue annually.

Organised after his death by the Worshipful Company of Fishmongers, and now raced from London Bridge to Cadogan Pier, the winner receives a traditional red watermen's coat with a distinctive silver badge – displaying the white horse of the House of Hanover and the word 'Liberty' – on the sleeve.

Intriguingly, this plaque records not only the founding of "the Race for Doggett's Coat and Badge" but also that "he died a pauper", which by all accounts he did not.

Doggett's enduring legacy is Britain's oldest boat race and probably the oldest continuously contested sporting event in the world. It is a lasting contribution to the capital's sporting heritage.

Right: A contemporary artist's painting, c1799, of the famous Race for Doggett's Coat and Badge

Below: The winners of each year's race traditionally participate in the Lord Mayor's Show in the City of London, parading their distinctive liveries

The Race for Doggett's Coat and Badge is probably the oldest continuously contested sporting event in the world

26

Blackheath Football Club

The Princess of Wales, Montpelier Row, Blackheath

SE3 0RL

In Blackheath, we stop by the heath at The Princess of Wales public house and reflect on the significant role played by Blackheath Football Club in sporting history. Founded by old boys from Blackheath Proprietary School in 1858, it opened its membership four years later and claims to be the oldest independent or 'open' rugby club in the world.

Blackheath was also a founder member of the Football Association in 1863 in the quest for a common set of rules for 'football'. The club soon, however, withdrew its membership when rules were proposed to remove 'hacking' (the practice of kicking or tripping an opponent). The club favoured a 'carrying and hacking' game. Representatives of Blackheath and like-minded teams subsequently met at the Pall Mall Restaurant in 1871 to establish the Rugby Football Union (*see Central London*).

Blackheath also helped organise the first international rugby match, held in Edinburgh in 1871. The leading Scottish clubs issued a challenge for a 20-a-side game versus England, and it was Blackheath which accepted, with club member 20-year-old Frederick Stokes becoming the first captain of the English national team. England's first home international match, against Wales in 1881, was later held here at Blackheath.

The Princess of Wales was used as the club's changing facilities and clubhouse. Inside, sadly no longer on public view following a recent refurbishment, two plaques for many years recorded the historical role of Blackheath Football Club. Now we can only look across the heath and imagine.

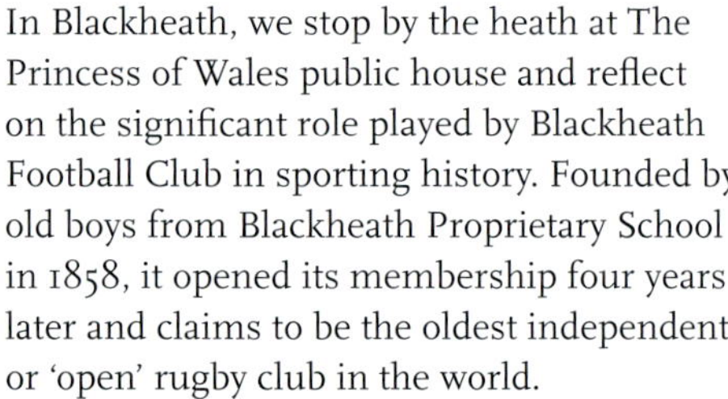

Right: A newspaper illustration records an England try against Wales at Blackheath FC's ground at Rectory Field in 1883

Below: The view across the historic heath from The Princess of Wales public house

SOUTH-EAST

THE ILLUSTRATED LONDON NEWS, Jan. 9, 1892.—40

INTERNATIONAL FOOTBALL: ENGLAND v. WALES.

THE MATCH AT BLACKHEATH.

Blackheath Football Club played a prominent role in rugby history

27

Sam Bartram

1914 – 1981

The Valley, Floyd Road, Charlton

SE7 8BL

Close to the main entrance of The Valley, Charlton Athletic's football ground, goalkeeper Sam Bartram stands in bronze as if about to stride out onto the pitch.

Bartram signed for the club in 1934 and was literally the first name on the team sheet for more than 20 years. The former miner had been scouted playing for his village team when he had only gone in goal as there was no one else available. He went on to play a record 623 games for Charlton and was never dropped. His acrobatic saves, distinctive sandy-coloured hair and genial smile endeared him to fans throughout the country.

During the club's centenary celebrations in 2005, this nine-feet-high statue of the club's legendary goalkeeper, sculpted by Anthony Hawken, was unveiled. The detail reveals the heavy, laced boots and prominent shin pads, the leathery ball in gnarled, weathered hands and a beaming smile from the Charlton legend to greet the crowd.

Sam Bartram stands in bronze as if about to stride out onto the pitch

28

Tom Cribb

1781 – 1848

St Mary's Gardens, John Wilson Street, Woolwich

SE18 6DU

We end our sporting tour of south-east London in Woolwich and in the churchyard of St Mary Magdalene Church. Here we find the resting place of Tom Cribb, the legendary bare-knuckle prize-fighter of the early 19th century.

Recalled earlier at the Tom Cribb public house in Panton Street (*see Central London*), Cribb moved to Woolwich when his fighting days as Champion of England were over. He worked as a baker with his son but his health soon declined. He is buried in the north-east corner of the churchyard. Here we discover a striking sculptural memorial tomb, funded by public subscription, which was erected to commemorate the great fighter.

Substantial and imposing, the stone monument is in the shape of a noble lion (an emblem of courage and fight) whose mane is flowing and whose paw is resting gently on an urn bearing the inscription: "Sacred to the memory of Thomas Cribb."

A lion grieves for a great prize-fighter

SOUTH-EAST

SET
SPORT
RBS

SOUTH-WEST LONDON

Twice winner of the singles at Wimbledon as well as Olympic champion, triumphs all achieved on the Centre Court in SW19, Andy Murray is one of Britain's finest sportsmen of the 21st century.

SOUTH-WEST LONDON

South-West London is the home of some of the world's great sporting venues. Twickenham is the spiritual home of rugby union, Wimbledon is famous worldwide for the oldest and most prestigious tennis championships, and Epsom has for more than two centuries provided a pilgrimage for Londoners to enjoy the Derby. Each venue radiates sporting history and rugby, tennis and horse-racing feature strongly here.

Other sports are also well represented in our circular tour of South-West London. In football, we come across the first official match of association football, the resting place of one of the game's 'founding fathers', and the recall of one of the game's stunning results. Venerated names associated with speed and motor sports are celebrated, as are two famous racehorses who join our renowned sporting heroes along with history's most famous greyhound. The early story of rowing is also represented, including a pioneer of women's rowing.

With other unexpected discoveries, South-West London is an area joyfully rich in sporting heritage.

1. The first match of association football
2. Ted 'Kid' Lewis
3. Jack Clasper
4. Steve Fairbairn
5. Ebenezer Cobb Morley
6. Amy Gentry
7. Kitty Godfree
8. Wimbledon: Worple Road
9. Sophie Hosking
10. Spencer Gore
11. Walter Wingfield
12. Fred Perry
13. Wimbledon: Britain's ladies' champions:
Kitty Godfree, Dorothy Round, Angela Mortimer, Ann Jones, Virginia Wade
14. Sir Andy Murray
15. Legends of Plough Lane:
Dave Beasant, Roy Law, Mick The Miller, Ronnie Moore,
16. Sir Charles Bunbury
17. Lester Piggott
18. AC Cars
19. Desert Orchid and Kauto Star
20. Sir Malcolm and Donald Campbell
21. Sir Mo Farah
22. Adrian Stoop
23. Nick Duncombe
24. George Rowland Hill
25. Twickenham – spirit of rugby

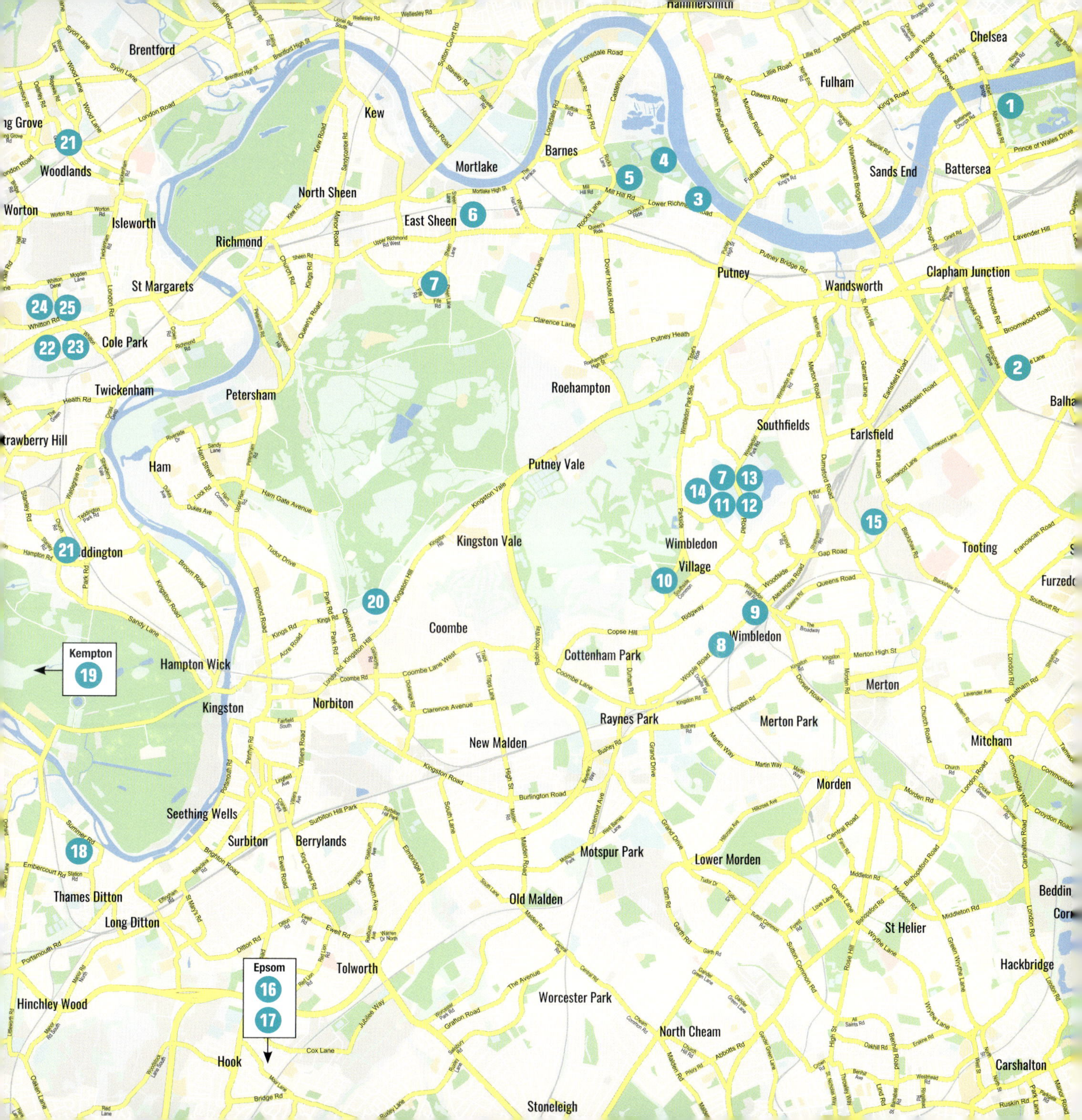
Hammersmith
Chelsea
Brentford
Fulham
Kew
Barnes
Mortlake
Sands End
Battersea
Woodlands
Worton
North Sheen
Isleworth
East Sheen
Richmond
Putney
Wandsworth
Clapham Junction
St Margarets
Cole Park
Twickenham
Petersham
Roehampton
Southfields
Earlsfield
Ham
Putney Vale
Kingston Vale
Wimbledon
Village
Tooting
Coombe
Cottenham Park
Kempton
Hampton Wick
Kingston
Norbiton
Raynes Park
Merton
Merton Park
New Malden
Mitcham
Morden
Seething Wells
Surbiton
Berrylands
Motspur Park
Lower Morden
Thames Ditton
Old Malden
Long Ditton
St Helier
Hackbridge
Epsom
Tolworth
Worcester Park
Hinchley Wood
North Cheam
Hook
Carshalton
Stoneleigh
1
2
3
4
5
6
7
8
9
10
11
12
13
14
15
16
17
18
19
20
21
22
23
24
25

1

The first match of association football

1864

Cricket Pavilion, Battersea Park, Battersea

SW11 4NJ

We begin our tour outside the cricket pavilion in Battersea Park, where a plaque recalls a landmark event that took place here on 9 January 1864.

Barely two months after the formation of the Football Association (FA) in October 1863 (*see Central London*), the FA arranged the first official match of association football. A plaque, erected by Wandsworth Council 150 years later in 2014, identifies the location of this historic occasion.

By December 1863, the members of the new association had agreed the basic rules to govern their newly formalised game. They arranged an exhibition match in Battersea Park to test and promote them. On a cold, icy morning, two 14-a-side teams took to the field, captained respectively by the FA President and the FA Secretary. The match was won 2-0 by the FA President's XIV, with both goals being scored by Charles Alcock (*see South-East London*). A contemporary report described the scene as "28 men in jerseys and knickerbockers whose appearance might be considered distinctly hipsterish".

At a dinner after the match, a toast was raised: "Success to football, irrespective of class or creed."

The old cricket pavilion in Battersea Park recalls the park's historic role in football

The first official match of association football was played here

SOUTH-WEST

2

Ted 'Kid' Lewis

1893 – 1970

Nightingale House, 105 Nightingale Lane, Wandsworth

SW12 8NB

We head to Wandsworth, where we discover the story of Ted 'Kid' Lewis. Born in a tenement in Whitechapel, Lewis (originally Gershon Mendeloff) became one of Britain's finest boxers and an international celebrity in the 1920s.

The story goes that, after seeing him brawling as a boy in the street, a police officer suggested the youth should take up boxing. At the age of 19 and fighting as 'Kid' Lewis, he became the youngest-ever British featherweight champion. Then, in 1915, he became world welterweight champion and the first British fighter to win a world title in the USA.

Confident, popular and well-connected (Charlie Chaplin was a close friend and godfather to his son), he fought in Australia, Canada and the USA, and briefly entered the world of Hollywood films in America, typecast (perhaps unsurprisingly) as a fighter. He was inducted into the International Boxing Hall of Fame in 1992.

Lewis spent his final years in Nightingale House, a residential home for the Jewish community by Wandsworth Common. It is here that a blue wall plaque was erected by English Heritage in 2003.

After seeing Lewis brawling in the street, a police officer suggested he take up boxing

Ted 'Kid' Lewis, the first British fighter to win a world title in the USA, poses for the camera

3

Jack Clasper

1836 – 1908

Westminster School Boat Club, Embankment, Putney

SW15 1LB

We move to the riverside at Putney, where we find the Westminster School Boat Club. On its brick frontage there is a reminder of a former occupant and the great rivalry between the watermen of the Thames led by Robert Coombes (*see West London*) and their counterparts on the River Tyne led by Harry Clasper.

Clasper was a legend in north-east England, known both as a racer and as a boat builder who introduced a radical redesign to the field of racing boats. Clasper's youngest son, John Hawkes Clasper – better known as 'Jack' – moved to London in 1854 and made his own name as an oarsman and boat builder. Like his father, he was forever experimenting with ways to produce better, faster watercraft – including with a form of sliding seat and longer, narrower shells – and multiple Clasper-built boats secured victory in the University Boat Race.

This boatyard, built by Jack in 1883, was taken over by Westminster School in 1921, but the family name lives on in its brickwork.

The Clasper name lives on here in Putney

A lithograph of legendary rower and boat builder Harry Clasper

SOUTH-WEST

Steve Fairbairn

1862 – 1938

Putney Towpath, Barn Elms, Embankment, Putney

SW13 8QZ

Staying on the southern riverbank of the Thames, exactly one mile from the start of the Championship Course for the University Boat Race, which is run from Putney to Mortlake, a stone obelisk – the Mile Post – bears a prominent portrait of Steve Fairbairn.

Born in Australia, Fairbairn went to Cambridge and rowed four times in the Boat Race in the 1880s. He later became an influential coach, his revolutionary approach to the sport encouraging his crews to slide in their seats to maximise leg-drive and stressing the importance of rowing with a flowing movement. In 1925, he founded the prestigious Head of the River Race, held annually on the Championship Course (albeit in the opposite direction to the Boat Race).

The Mile Post permanently commemorates one of the sport's major figures at a significant location beside the historic river. For many, Steve Fairbairn is the father of modern rowing.

Steve Fairbairn is, for many, the father of modern rowing

5

Ebenezer Cobb Morley

1831 – 1924

Barnes Old Cemetery,
Rocks Lane, Barnes

SW13 9SA

We have paid tribute earlier *(see Central London)* to the role of Ebenezer Cobb Morley in the formation of the Football Association in 1863 and the game's early development. It was the Yorkshire-born solicitor and sportsman who led the drafting of the first rules of association football.

In a secluded area near a clearing on the east side of the wooded and now disused Barnes Old Cemetery, Morley's previously overgrown grave was renovated in 2015 as part of the 150th anniversary celebrations of the formation of the Football Association. It was the scene of a wreath laid in 2024 on the centenary of his death.

6

Amy Gentry OBE

1903 – 1976

29 Thornton Road, East Sheen

SW14 8NS

Rowing was for very many years a male-dominated sport. However, a visit to East Sheen unveils the story of Amy Gentry who was a pioneering figure in the emergence of women's rowing.

Born in Barnes, Gentry started rowing at Weybridge Rowing Club. In 1926, she founded the separate – and still thriving – Weybridge Ladies Amateur Rowing Club to provide suitable coaching and equipment for herself and other female rowers. A fierce competitor, she was Britain's undefeated women's single scull champion in 1932, 1933 and 1934. She then became a successful administrator, making a significant contribution to the sport's development as well as acting as the secretary of – and later chairing – the Women's Committee of the Amateur Rowing Association.

Gentry sadly died in 1976, just two weeks before a Weybridge ladies' four represented Great Britain in Montreal –

Right: Amy Gentry receives the British women's single sculls trophy in 1932

women's rowing having finally been added to the Olympic programme. It has since become a sport in which Britain has enjoyed much international success.

Employed by Vickers-Armstrongs during the Second World War, Gentry was personal secretary to Barnes Wallis when he was developing his innovative bouncing bomb, which would famously destroy two dams during the 'Dambusters' raid. Once, while out on a rowing boat on Silvermere Lake in Surrey when Wallis was testing various models of his creation, she forcefully took command to ensure they did not capsize, saying: "Sit down Wallis! You'll have us both in the water, and I'm in charge of this boat."

For a time, a plastic plaque was placed on the front gate of Gentry's former home in Thornton Road. Featured here, it is now kept inside. A blue English Heritage plaque may be considered for this pioneer of women's rowing.

Amy Gentry was a pioneer of women's rowing

7

Kitty Godfree

1896 – 1992

55 York Avenue, East Sheen

SW14 7LQ

The All England Lawn Tennis Club, Church Road, Wimbledon

SW19 5AE

Still in East Sheen, we move to tennis – a sport associated worldwide with south-west London – and discover the former home of two-time Wimbledon winner and the first great British player in the decade after the First World War, Kathleen ('Kitty') Godfree, née McKane. A plaque erected in 2006 by English Heritage marks the location.

Excelling also at badminton, her greatest lawn tennis triumph came in 1924 when she beat the American Helen Wills in the Wimbledon ladies' singles final. Two years later and now married, she won again. She also reached the singles finals at both the US and the French championships in 1925, becoming the first woman to reach three different 'Grand Slam' finals in her career. Tennis was then an Olympic sport and, at Antwerp 1920 and Paris 1924, Kitty won five Olympic medals – a record for a tennis player only matched (much later) by Venus Williams – including a gold in the ladies' doubles in 1920. In 1926, Godfree and her husband, Leslie, became the first – and so far only – husband-and-wife pair to win the mixed doubles title at Wimbledon.

Fondly remembered in East Sheen, where she lived for more than 50 years, in later life she would often be seen happily riding her bicycle around the local lanes. At the All England Lawn Tennis Club a few miles away, Godfree was the first of five British ladies' singles champions since the move to the present grounds in 1922 to be immortalised in bronze (*see page 224*).

Kitty McKane (later Godfree) in action in 1923 at Wimbledon – a year later she would be champion

SOUTH-WEST

In later life she would often be seen happily riding her bicycle around the local lanes

8

Wimbledon: Worple Road

Nursery Road, Wimbledon

SW19 4JA

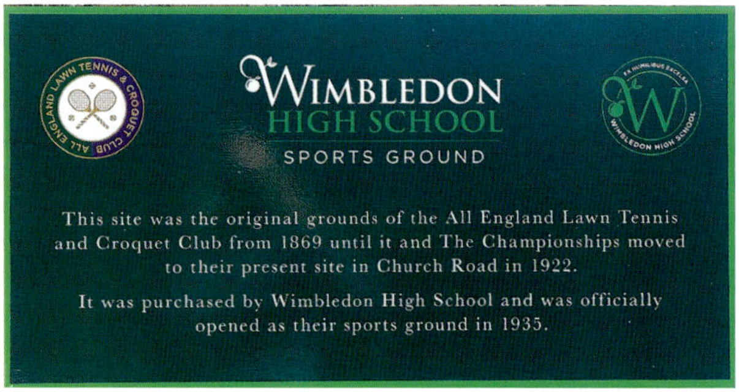

WIMBLEDON
HIGH SCHOOL
SPORTS GROUND

This site was the original grounds of the All England Lawn Tennis and Croquet Club from 1869 until it and The Championships moved to their present site in Church Road in 1922.

It was purchased by Wimbledon High School and was officially opened as their sports ground in 1935.

Arriving in Wimbledon itself, we discover the original home of the All England Club in Nursery Road, off Worple Road, which now accommodates the playing fields of Wimbledon High School.

The All England Croquet Club, formed in 1868, found initial grounds here beside the local railway line. Seven years later, the decision was taken to convert a croquet lawn into a court for the newly popular game of lawn tennis. Then, in 1877, the world's first Lawn Tennis Championship was held here. The grounds became synonymous internationally with the sport and hosted the lawn tennis event at the London Olympic Games of 1908.

After the First World War, the facilities were unable to cope with spectator demand and a new site was found elsewhere in Wimbledon. There was some sadness and concern at the move in 1922, with *Lawn Tennis & Badminton* declaring: "The fame of the present venue is worldwide: to forsake it might be dangerous." Happily, that proved not to be the case.

A plaque erected in 2012 by the local council and the All England Club commemorates this site's momentous history.

Arriving in Wimbledon, we discover the original home of the All England Club

A vintage photograph of the original Centre Court at Worple Road in 1884, synonymous with tennis until 1922

9

Sophie Hosking MBE

1986 –

Worple Road, Wimbledon

SW19 4DP

Travelling along Worple Road towards the centre of Wimbledon, outside Elys department store a gold-painted Royal Mail post box honours local rower Sophie Hosking. Alongside Kat Copeland, she won an unexpected but glorious gold medal in the women's lightweight double sculls at the London 2012 Games – the first British triumph on the day that became 'Super Saturday'. Fans of AFC Wimbledon Women may also recall that Hosking was a midfielder for the local football team.

Sophie Hosking (rear) wins Olympic gold with Kat Copeland in 2012

10

Spencer Gore

1850 – 1906

Westside House, West Side Common, Wimbledon

SW19 4UD

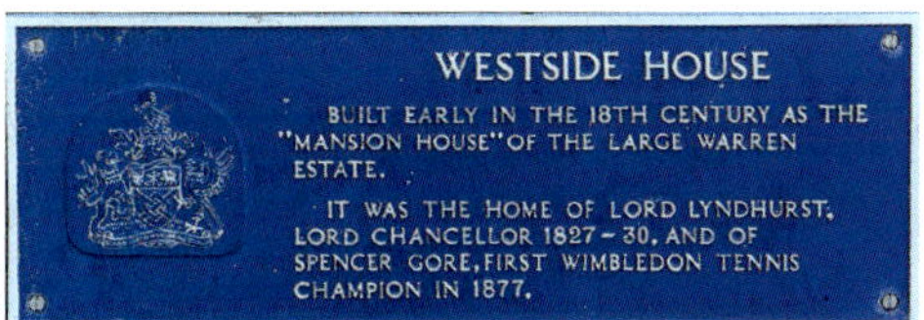

Spencer Gore was the winner of the first Lawn Tennis Championship in 1877. Gore had played rackets and real tennis at Harrow before he entered the new tournament at Wimbledon as a member of the 22-player gentlemen's singles draw, paying one guinea to enter.

Gore duly made it to the final – held after a two-day break while the annual Eton vs Harrow cricket match was played at Lord's. With some effective volleying, Gore won the final in three straight sets. He played again the following year but lost narrowly in the Challenge Round and Wimbledon did not see him again.

Now, on the boundary wall at Westside House, a plaque records the fact that Spencer Gore is amongst the residence's notable former occupants.

11

Walter Wingfield

1833 – 1912

Wimbledon Lawn Tennis Museum,
Church Road, Wimbledon

SW19 5AE

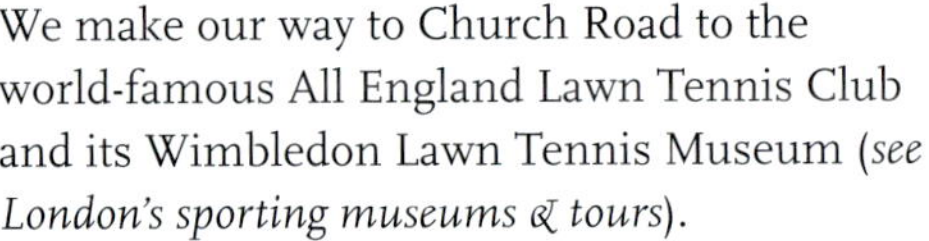

We make our way to Church Road to the world-famous All England Lawn Tennis Club and its Wimbledon Lawn Tennis Museum (*see London's sporting museums & tours*).

The first stop is to pay further tribute to Walter Wingfield. Wingfield, an inventor and entrepreneur, had seen the opportunity to introduce a summer garden sport more energetic than croquet but which could still be played by both sexes. It was his invention in 1874 of a portable tennis court and equipment, and his promotional skills, which created the game that swept through the English-speaking world.

We have already featured Wingfield's former home in Pimlico (*see Central London*) and his founding contribution to the game. The All England Club may have introduced many changes for the first Championship in 1877, but it was Wingfield's court and equipment that started it all.

Fittingly, a fine bronze bust of Wingfield, sculpted by Albert Toft, can be found in the Wimbledon Lawn Tennis Museum. Beside it is the gravestone of his Pekinese dog, Joss, faithfully brought home from China following Wingfield's service in a Dragoon Guards regiment of the British Army.

Above: Wingfield's boxed set for lawn tennis which was patented in 1874

Below: The gravestone of Wingfield's faithful dog, Joss

Right: The portrait bust of Major Walter Wingfield in the Wimbledon Lawn Tennis Museum

SOUTH-WEST

Wingfield created the game that swept through the English-speaking world

12

Fred Perry

1909 – 1995

The All England Lawn Tennis Club, Church Road, Wimbledon

SW19 5AE

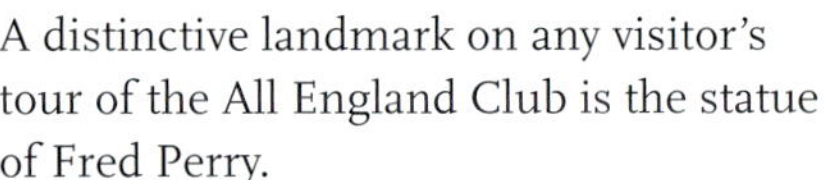

A distinctive landmark on any visitor's tour of the All England Club is the statue of Fred Perry.

Perry was the finest British men's tennis player of the 20th century – a three-time Wimbledon singles champion and leader of Great Britain's triumphant Davis Cup team in the 1930s. It would be another 77 years before a British male player would emulate his feat of winning the singles at Wimbledon.

Born into a working-class background in Stockport, Perry developed first as a table-tennis player before turning to lawn tennis and becoming the dominant player of his age. In addition to his Wimbledon titles, he triumphed in the US, French and Australian championships and was the first man to complete a 'career Grand Slam' by winning all four major singles titles. Perry's leap over the net after match point demonstrated not only his fitness but his sense of theatre. He was a champion.

A plaque erected in Ealing in 2012 by English Heritage celebrates Fred Perry's London home (*see West London*), where we have addressed his career more fully.

Here, at the All England Lawn Tennis Club, to celebrate the 50th anniversary of Perry's first Wimbledon title, a three-quarter life-size statue was commissioned from sculptor David Wynne. Perry himself was present at the unveiling in 1984. The statue has a prominent position in front of the Centre Court, showing Perry's sweeping forehand ready to strike.

Above: Fred Perry jumps the net on his way to Wimbledon success in 1936

Below and right: Fred Perry's statue stands prominently in front of the Centre Court he graced

Fred Perry was the finest British men's tennis player of the 20th century

13

Wimbledon: Britain's ladies' champions

The All England Lawn Tennis Club, Church Road, Wimbledon

SW19 5AE

The ivy-clad frontage of the famous Centre Court is the setting for bronze portrait busts – created by sculptor Ian Rank-Broadley – of the five British women who have won the Wimbledon ladies' singles title since the All England Club's move to its present site in 1922.

The first was **Kitty Godfree** (1896–1992) (*see also page 216*). Britain's other two-time winner between the First and Second World Wars was **Dorothy Round** (1909–1982). Born in Worcestershire, Round was a Sunday School teacher and also a resolute competitor. Her two title victories in SW19 came in 1934 and 1937.

On the other side of the club's entrance are busts depicting the three winners since the Second World War. The first, in 1961, was Devon's **Angela Mortimer MBE** (1932–2025). It was even an all-British ladies' final at Wimbledon when Mortimer edged out Essex's Christine Truman in a tense three-set match. The second home ladies' singles winner in the 1960s was Warwickshire's **Ann Jones CBE** (1938–). Aged 30, Jones achieved her Wimbledon singles' triumph in 1969, defeating the defending champion, Billie-Jean King, in the final.

Virginia Wade raises the ladies' singles trophy beside Queen Elizabeth II in 1977

SOUTH-WEST

The third was **Virginia Wade OBE** (1945–). "For she's a jolly good fellow" rang out around Centre Court in 1977 as Wade received the trophy from Queen Elizabeth II in her Silver Jubilee year after clinching the ladies' singles title. Wade's tennis career spanned the end of the amateur era and the game becoming 'open' to professionals in 1968. Her portrait bust bears a warm and gentle smile.

Left: Kitty Godfree (left) and Virginia Wade, both winners at Wimbledon, together at the Champions' Dinner in 1990

14

Sir Andy Murray

1987 –

Somerset Road, Wimbledon

SW19 7HU

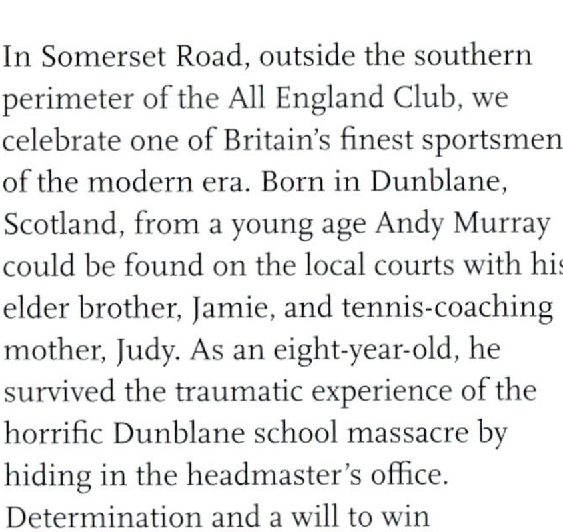

In Somerset Road, outside the southern perimeter of the All England Club, we celebrate one of Britain's finest sportsmen of the modern era. Born in Dunblane, Scotland, from a young age Andy Murray could be found on the local courts with his elder brother, Jamie, and tennis-coaching mother, Judy. As an eight-year-old, he survived the traumatic experience of the horrific Dunblane school massacre by hiding in the headmaster's office. Determination and a will to win would fuel a great career.

Just weeks after emotionally losing to Roger Federer in the Wimbledon final, Murray's major breakthrough came in the summer of 2012 when he defeated Federer on the same Centre Court to win the gold medal at the London Olympics. This was followed, in the same year, by his first 'Grand Slam' title at the US Open. When he won Wimbledon in 2013, the 26-year-old Scot became the first British men's singles champion at Wimbledon for 77 years.

Triumphing at Wimbledon again in 2016, his record of three Grand Slam titles, along with heading GB's 2015 Davis Cup-winning team, retaining his Olympic title in 2016 and finishing 2016 as the world No.1 ranked

A golden champion, Andy Murray has cemented his place in British sporting history

A gold-painted post box, with the grounds of the All England Club behind, commemorates Andy Murray's 2012 Olympic triumph

player, has cemented his place in British sporting history.

A distinctive portrait of Murray by artist Maggi Hambling hangs in the National Portrait Gallery, and a statue is planned at the All England Club. In the meantime, a gold-painted post box, honouring his Olympic gold medal in 2012, can be found here.

Andy Murray sinks to his knees in triumph on Centre Court in 2013

15

Legends of Plough Lane

Cherry Red Records Stadium, Plough Lane, Wimbledon

SW17 0NR

Plough Lane in Wimbledon was once the site of two sports stadiums – one for greyhound racing and later speedway, and the other the football home of Wimbledon FC. Now, rising from the site of the old greyhound arena, stands a fine new stadium for AFC Wimbledon, where sculptures commissioned by Wimbledon in Sporting History celebrate the site's distinctive history.

First, we recall Wimbledon FC's memorable victory in the FA Cup final in 1988. Having been playing non-league football just 11 years previously, Wimbledon faced league champions Liverpool at Wembley and won 1-0 in one of the competition's most stunning upsets. Goalkeeper and captain **Dave Beasant** (1959-) became the first man to save a penalty in an FA Cup final, before lifting the trophy.

Having departed Plough Lane in 1991, the club controversially moved to Milton Keynes in 2002. A new supporter-run team, AFC Wimbledon, rose from the ashes and in 2020 the club 'returned home' to Plough Lane. Outside the new stadium, an unusual wood-carved sculpture was erected in 2022 and celebrates that famous 1988 victory and Wimbledon's other cup win at Wembley, in the FA Amateur Cup in 1963 under long-serving captain **Roy Law** (1937–2014). The two cup-winning captains stand back-to-back.

Dave Beasant became the first man to save a penalty in an FA Cup final

Left: Wimbledon goalkeeper Dave Beasant writes his name into the history books at Wembley in 1988

SOUTH-WEST

Greyhound racing thrived at the original stadium and one dog, **Mick The Miller** (1926-1939), captured the public's affection like no other. Having won the 1929 English Greyhound Derby at White City, by claiming victory again in 1930 he became the first dog to win the race twice. Kennelled nearby, Mick The Miller appeared frequently at Wimbledon. Saved from the old stadium and, restored with support from the National Lottery Heritage Fund, a mosaic of this iconic greyhound now stands at the entrance to the new stadium as a tribute to this canine superstar.

Large crowds also flocked to Plough Lane in the 1950s and '60s for speedway, not least to watch two-time world champion **Ronnie Moore MBE** (1933–2018), a New Zealander who raced for 'The Dons' for more than 20 years. An extraordinary sculpture, made in 2025 from recycled speedway motorcycle parts by Jason Heppenstall, honours this legendary star.

Reminders of past heroes on the Wimbledon track – greyhound Mick The Miller (top right) and speedway star Ronnie Moore as a 17-year-old (top left) and now in metal (above)

16

Sir Charles Bunbury

1740 – 1821

Market Square, Epsom

KT18 5BY

We move out to Epsom. Sir Charles Bunbury was a major force behind horse-racing's Derby. As Steward of the Jockey Club (formed in 1750) and 'Dictator of the Turf', Bunbury pioneered major changes to the sport, including shorter races for fast, younger horses. As a result, the first 'Classics' were established – including the Derby.

It was in Woodmansterne, not far from Epsom, that the Derby was conceived at a dinner party hosted at the Earl of Derby's country house to celebrate the successful staging of the Oaks Stakes for three-year old fillies in 1779. The story is that Bunbury and the Earl of Derby resolved that a new race for three-year old colts and fillies should be held over a mile at Epsom. The honour of naming the race would be decided by a toss of a coin between the Earl and Bunbury. The Earl won. There was consolation for Bunbury, however, in that the first winner of the Derby Stakes, in 1780, was his fine horse, Diomed, who was named after the Greek hero.

The Derby – now run over a mile and a half – soon became the sport's most prestigious Classic, with racing fans congregating annually on Epsom Downs for a mix of sport and festival.

In Epsom's Market Square, a striking sculpture entitled 'Evocation of Speed' features Diomed racing against the outstanding winner of 2001, Galileo. Sculpted by Judy Boyt and originally installed in 2001, it reflects the notable difference in riding styles of jockeys over the ages. Charles Bunbury would have relished the long-term success of the Derby.

Sir Charles Bunbury was the first 'Dictator of the Turf'

Right: Bunbury's Diomed (foreground), the first winner of the Derby, races Galileo, winner in 2001, in an impressive bronze sculpture

SOUTH-WEST

17

Lester Piggott

1935 – 2022

Epsom Downs Racecourse, Epsom

KT18 5LQ

Above: Painted panels at Epsom depict Lester Piggott's extraordinary life in racing

Lester Piggott is probably the greatest and most popular flat-racing jockey of all time. With nine Derby winners, his mastery of the Epsom racecourse was unparalleled.

The son of a successful National Hunt jockey and trainer, Piggott was born into racing. His first Derby winner came when he was aged just 18. For the public, he was 'the' name, a jockey who dominated the people's attention and affection and whose very presence added excitement to any race. For racing connoisseurs, he combined the best of racing skills with an obsessive will to win. Champion jockey 11 times with a record 30 domestic Classic winners, Piggott retired for the final time in 1994.

At Epsom racecourse, 'the Lester Piggott Gates' were dedicated in his honour and unveiled by Queen Elizabeth II in 1996. Two circular panels on the gates incorporate paintings by artist Roy Miller commemorating the legendary jockey's triumphs at Epsom in its greatest races – the Derby, the Oaks and the Coronation Cup. His winners are a roll call of great racehorses.

The Jockey Club later marked Piggott's contribution to British horse racing with a statue of the 'Long Fellow', by sculptor William Newton, that was placed at nine major courses. The first was unveiled here at Epsom by Queen Elizabeth II on the 65th anniversary of Lester Piggott's first Derby win.

Below: Queen Elizabeth II unveils the statue of Piggott at Epsom in 2019

SOUTH-WEST

Lester Piggott is probably the greatest and most popular flat-racing jockey of all time

AC Cars

Ashley Road, Thames Ditton

KT7 0SA

AC CARS LIMITED FIRST OCCUPIED THIS SITE
IN 1911
AND
IT WAS FROM HERE THAT THE FAMOUS COBRA WAS DEVELOPED
IN 1963.
INSPIRED BY THE AMERICAN CARROL SHELBY, THE CAR WAS
GENERALLY ACKNOWLEDGED TO BE ONE OF THE FASTEST
TWO-SEATER PRODUCTION SPORTS CARS IN THE WORLD.
IT WENT ON TO ACHIEVE FAME GLOBALLY IN SUCH
GLORIOUS RACES AS
THE
24-HOUR LE MANS, THE MILLE MIGLIA
AND THE
TARGA FLORIA.

Heading back towards London, we stop just off the High Street in Thames Ditton, near the River Thames. Here was the headquarters of AC Cars, formerly Auto Carriers Limited, a famous name (with its iconic roundel logo) in the development of sports cars.

Founded in 1901 by the Weller Brothers in West Norwood, the company is said to be Britain's oldest active vehicle manufacturer. Its most famous model is the AC Cobra, originally developed in cooperation with famous American designer and entrepreneur Carroll Shelby and Ford, who provided the car's V8 engine. The legendary car was first produced in 1962 here in the company's Ferry Works factory, occupied by AC between 1911 and 1979.

The Cobra, a modern version of which is still manufactured by the company (now based in Donington), is generally acknowledged to be one of the fastest two-seater production sports cars in the world.

During its heyday in the 1960s, the AC Cobra was driven to famous victories in both the iconic 24 Hours of Le Mans and Mille Miglia sports car races.

An AC Cobra-Ford in the pits during the 24 Hours of Le Mans race in 1963

The 'AC' name is legendary in the world of sports cars

19

Desert Orchid and Kauto Star

Kempton Park Racecourse,
Staines Road East,
Sunbury-on-Thames

TW16 5AQ

Desert Orchid (foreground) and Kauto Star in bronze and still in the limelight at Kempton Park

Although facing an uncertain future, Kempton Park still offers, at the time of writing, the opportunity to enjoy in bronze two of the outstanding racehorses to grace this historic racecourse.

Desert Orchid (1979–2006), just 'Dessie' to millions of fans, was one of the best-loved racehorses of his era. It was here, annually on Boxing Day before huge crowds, that the distinctive grey ran in six consecutive King George VI Chase races, winning first in 1986 and then three times in a row from 1988 to 1990. He also, thrillingly, won the 1989 Cheltenham Gold Cup. Now Dessie stands resplendent in a statue, by sculptor Philip Blacker and unveiled in 1991, in a lawned setting overlooking the parade ring.

Kauto Star (2000–2015), strong and with a distinctive white blaze on the head, was similarly much loved by racegoers to Kempton Park, where he won the King George VI Chase a record five times. One of the all-time great steeplechasers, Kauto Star also won the Cheltenham Gold Cup twice. In 2014, a fine statue by leading equine sculptor Charlie Langton was unveiled inside the parade ring. Kauto Star, in attendance at the unveiling, glanced with approval.

Great racehorses provide vivid memories. We celebrate here, at Kempton Park, two supreme equine heroes.

Dessie and Kauto Star, still in the limelight at Kempton Park

20

Sir Malcolm Campbell and Donald Campbell CBE

1885 – 1948 & 1921 – 1967

Canbury School, Kingston Hill, Kingston upon Thames

KT2 7LN

A plaque erected by English Heritage in 2010 at Canbury School in Kingston Hill, which was converted from a family residence, celebrates Malcolm and Donald Campbell – a legendary father and son pairing among British racers who were relentless in the pursuit of speed on land and water.

This was the home of Malcolm and the birthplace of his son, Donald. Between the two of them, they claimed 10 speed records on land and 11 on water. Malcolm set the first of his land speed records in 1924 and the last, topping 300 mph, in 1935. Subsequently, he achieved record speeds on water four times. He was knighted in 1931.

Malcolm Campbell and his son, Donald, between them set more than 20 land and water speed records

Donald carried on the family tradition and became the fastest on land in 1964, then achieved the unique feat of breaking the water speed record in the same year. It was during a further attempt on the water speed record, on Coniston Water in the Lake District, that he was tragically killed three years later.

Malcolm Campbell looks on as his young son Donald sits proudly in the new 'Bluebird' in 1933

SOUTH-WEST

21

Sir Mo Farah

1983 –

477 London Road, Isleworth

TW7 4BX

Broad Street, Teddington

TW11 8RF

Born in Somalia and (it has been revealed) trafficked to the UK aged nine, Mo Farah became one of the most successful distance runners of all time.

Forced to work as a servant for a local family, he nevertheless attended Feltham Community College and then Isleworth & Syon School for his sixth form years, where his prowess as a runner became apparent. Greatness lay ahead. A (sadly now fading) gold-painted post box outside the Isleworth post office celebrates Farah's stunning victory in the 10,000m at the London 2012 Olympics when, with blistering pace, he burst clear for gold. Some 80,000 spectators and a nation of viewers and listeners were ecstatic.

Mo Farah became one of Britain's greatest athletes

Another golden post box (*right*), in Teddington on the corner of Broad Street and North Lane, celebrates Farah's 5000m success, which came a few days later on the same track. Farah lived for many years in Teddington, training with Kenyan athletes at the nearby St Mary University's performance centre. Gloriously, he repeated this outstanding distance 'double' at the 2016 Rio Olympics, as well as winning World Championship titles in both events.

Above: Mo Farah is victorious in the 5000m at the 2012 Olympics

SOUTH-WEST

Adrian Stoop

1883 – 1957

The Twickenham Stoop,
Langhorn Drive, Twickenham

TW2 7SX

Above: Lieutenant Stoop, British Army Officer

Above left: Adrian Stoop in 1911 at Harlequins, for whom he played 182 times and later served as president for 30 years

In Twickenham, we head first to the home of Harlequins Rugby Club. Acquired in 1963 and initially named the Stoop Memorial Ground, it is formally now The Twickenham Stoop. For most fans it is simply 'The Stoop'.

The ground is named in memory of Adrian Stoop, who was born in Kensington of a Dutch father and British mother and made a major contribution to rugby union in the early 20th century. He led Harlequins for eight years before the First World War as it became the country's leading club side. He debuted for England in 1905 and earned 15 caps, captaining the national team in the first-ever international played at Twickenham in 1910. Stoop is widely credited with transforming free-flowing back play – developing the structure of scrum-half and fly-half, rather than two half-backs, and bringing great success to both club and country.

Awarded the Military Cross during the war for "conspicuous gallantry and devotion to duty", he returned to lead Harlequins and help restore national pride in the game he loved.

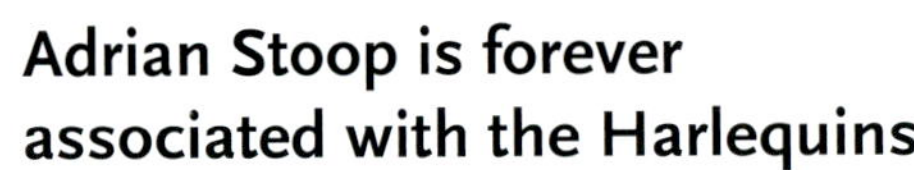

Adrian Stoop is forever associated with the Harlequins

23

Nick Duncombe

1982 – 2003

The Twickenham Stoop, Langhorn Drive, Twickenham

TW2 7SX

Staying at The Stoop, we move forward to a different generation. Nick Duncombe was a highly promising scrum-half for Harlequins. He made his England debut aged just 20, and a long international future seemingly lay ahead. Aged just 21, however, Duncombe died in 2003 having contracted meningitis whilst on holiday. Then-England coach Clive Woodward paid a moving tribute: "Nick was one of our brightest and most talented players in the game". A statue by sculptor Nathan David commemorates a life and career tragically cut short.

24

Sir George Rowland Hill

1855 – 1928

Allianz Stadium, Whitton Road, Twickenham

TW2 7BA

KEITH WILLIAMS/CREATIVECOMMONS

We move on to the historic Twickenham Stadium itself (formally the Allianz Stadium since 2024).

At the main gateway to the West Stand, set within a stone pillar, a sculptural relief depicts the Greenwich-born Sir George Rowland Hill (*right*). Honorary secretary of the Rugby Football Union (RFU) from 1881 to 1904, Hill led the RFU's staunch refusal to countenance 'broken time' payments (principally sought by northern clubs) to cover a player's lost earnings during time spent training and playing rugby. Rugby, under the RFU, at this time remained strictly amateur. The RFU's refusal led to the formation of the professional rugby league in 1895 by breakaway clubs. Hill subsequently became president of the RFU, and in 1926 became the first man to be knighted for services to the game.

In 1995, a century after the breakaway, the world had changed fundamentally and the RFU finally accepted professionalism.

25

Twickenham – spirit of rugby

Allianz Stadium, Whitton Road, Twickenham

TW2 7BA

England's Martin Johnson wins another line-out against Australia in the 2003 Rugby World Cup final

We end by reflecting on the spirit of sport and its compelling features – the challenge of the contest, striving for success and sense of achievement – that have motivated athletes through the ages. A trip to Twickenham is a visit to the spiritual home of the sport. The World Rugby Museum situated in the South Stand (*see London's sporting museums & tours*) holds the largest collection of rugby memorabilia in the world.

Around the stadium are various generic sculptures acclaiming the spirit of rugby. Most notably, in 2010 the RFU installed a 27-feet tall, dramatic sculpture by Gerald Laing to greet spectators arriving at the plaza outside the South Stand. Depicting a line-out, engraved around the plinth are statements of five core values of the game – Teamwork, Respect, Enjoyment, Discipline and Sportsmanship.

Although generic, for many it celebrates England's World Cup victory in 2003. It was fitting, then, that Martin Johnson – towering lock forward, key line-out jumper and captain of England's World Cup team – was present at the unveiling. Barely reaching the waists of the standing players in bronze, he looked up. Will the catcher take the ball cleanly? In 2003, Johnson certainly won it for England.

In 2003, Martin Johnson certainly won the ball for England

BRITISH AIRWAYS
WELC
VIRGIN ACTIVE
HEALTH CLUB

London's sporting museums & tours

London's rich sporting heritage can be further enjoyed through a number of excellent museums and tours found at sports venues around the capital. Here is a directory of the most notable. Please note that dates and times of opening and availability should always be checked before any visit.

AFC Wimbledon Museum & Stadium Tour
Cherry Red Records Stadium
Plough lane
Wimbledon
London SW17 0NR
www.afcwimbledon.co.uk
Underground stations: Wimbledon, Wimbledon Park and Tooting Broadway
Rail stations: Wimbledon or Earlsfield

The Arsenal Museum & Stadium Tour
Emirates Stadium
Hornsey Road
London N7 7AJ
www.arsenal.com
Underground stations: Arsenal, Holloway Road or Finsbury Park

Brentford FC Stadium Tour
Gtech Community Stadium
Lionel Road South
Brentford
London TW8 0RU
www.brentfordfc.com
Underground station: Gunnersbury
Rail Station: Kew Bridge

Brooklands Museum of British Motorsport
Brooklands Drive
Weybridge
Surrey KT13 0SL
www.brooklandsmuseum.com
Rail station: Weybridge

Chelsea FC Museum & Stadium Tour
Stamford Bridge
Fulham Road
London SW6 1HS
www.chelseafc.com
Underground station: Fulham Broadway

Crystal Palace FC Stadium Tour
Selhurst Park,
Holmesdale Road
London SE25 6PU
www.cpfc.co.uk
Rail stations: Selhurst, Thornton Heath or Norwood Junction

This way to the popular Chelsea FC Museum & Stadium Tour

The MCC Museum at Lord's is worthy of its historic location

Fulham FC & Craven Cottage Tours
Craven Cottage
Stevenage Road
London SW6 6HH
www.fulhamfc.com
Underground station: Putney Bridge

Kia Oval Ground Tours & Galadari Museum
The Kia Oval
Surrey County Cricket Club
Kennington
London SE11 5SS
www.kiaoval.com
Underground station: Oval
Rail station: Vauxhall

Leyton Orient FC Stadium Tour
BetWright Stadium
Brisbane Road
Leyton
London E10 5NF
www.leytonorient.com
Underground station: Leyton

Marylebone Cricket Club Museum & Lord's Tour
Marylebone Cricket Club
Lord's Cricket Ground
St John's Wood Road
London NW8 8QN
www.lords.org
Underground station: St John's Wood

continues

London's sporting museums & tours

continued

Tottenham Hotspur Heritage Trail & Stadium Tour
High Road,
London N17 0BX
www.tottenhamhotspur.com
Underground station: Seven Sisters or Tottenham Hale
Rail station: White Hart Lane

Wembley Stadium Tour
Wembley Stadium
London HA9 0WS
www.wembleytours.com
Underground stations: Wembley Park or Wembley Central
Rail station: Wembley Stadium

Wimbledon Lawn Tennis Museum & Tour
Church Road
Wimbledon
London SW19 5AE
(use SW19 5AG for sat-nav)
www.wimbledon.com
Underground station: Southfields
Rail station: Wimbledon

World Rugby Museum & Twickenham Stadium Tour
Rugby Road
Twickenham Stadium
London TW1 1DZ
www.worldrugbymuseum.com
Rail station: Twickenham

Visitors to the Wimbledon Lawn Tennis Museum are taken on a journey right back to the roots of the game

Index

Excluding London's sporting museums & tours

Index

continued

Acknowledgements

Discovering London's sporting plaques and memorials has been a pleasurable task greatly assisted by two excellent database websites, namely those of London Remembers (*londonremembers.com*) and Plaques of London (*plaquesoflondon.co.uk*). They cover, respectively, memorials and plaques of all kinds in the capital. I would also mention English Heritage (*english-heritage.org.uk*) and its database of London's blue plaques. Each of these is informative, searchable by category and descriptive of locations – and invaluable for my purpose.

Any study of London's sporting heritage must pay tribute to Simon Inglis' magisterial work, *Played in London*, for English Heritage. A detailed history of London's sporting venues and architecture, past and existing, it is a foundational and inspiring work. As to the historical and social perspective of sport in this country, Richard Holt's preeminent *Sport and the British* and David Horspool's *More Than A Game* are outstanding.

In summarising individual 'heroes', I have inevitably drawn on a variety of websites, biographies, sporting anthologies and other sources. Any inaccuracies are my responsibility.

I am very grateful to Jim, Toby, Doug and Ed at Vision Sports Publishing for their creativity and patience in designing and putting this book together – and, as ever, to my wife Jenifer for her insight and vital encouragement.

Ian Hewitt, March 2026

About the author

Ian Hewitt was a partner in a leading international law firm. Also a former county tennis player, he was chairman of the All England Club, Wimbledon, from 2019 to 2023 and was awarded an MBE in 2024 for services to tennis and charity. He plays social golf and is a lifelong supporter of Southampton FC (both pursuits requiring optimism).

His sports book titles as author or co-author, all with Vision Sports Publishing, include: *Centre Court: The Jewel in Wimbledon's Crown* (4th ed. 2022) and *Wimbledon: Visions of The Championships* (2011) – both winners of the Best Illustrated Book Award at the British Sports Book Awards – and *Immortals of British Sport: A celebration of Britain's sporting history through sculpture* (2013).

He is a member of the British Society of Sports History and lives in London with his wife Jenifer.